Kinship in Bengali Culture

Kinship in Bengali Culture

Ronald B. Inden and Ralph W. Nicholas

University of Chicago Press

Chicago and London

The University of Chicago Press, Chicago 60637
The University of Chicago Press, Ltd., London

Printed in the United States of America
81 80 79 78 77 9 8 7 6 5 4 3 2 1

RONALD B. INDEN is associate professor of history at the University of Chicago. He is the author of *Marriage and Rank in Bengali Culture: A History of Caste and Clan in Middle-Period Bengal.*

RALPH W. NICHOLAS is professor of anthropology and of the social sciences in the College at the University of Chicago. He is the editor of the *Journal of Asian Studies*.

Library of Congress Cataloging in Publication Data

Inden, Ronald B
Kinship in Bengali culture.

Bibliography: p.
Includes index.
1. Kinship—Bengal. 2. Bengal—Social life and customs. I. Nichols, Ralph W., joint author. II. Title.
GN635.B46I53 301.42'1'095492 76-25639
ISBN 0-226-37835-7

To our Bengali friends

Contents

List of Illustrations viii

Acknowledgments ix

Introduction xi

1. *Ātmīya-svajana:* One's Own People 3
2. *Saṃskāra*s: The Generation and Transformation of the Body 35
3. Bengali Kinship Terminology 67

Conclusion 85

Appendixes
1. An Indigenous Account of Kinship 94
2. Bengali Muslim Kinship 99
3. Periods of Death and Birth Impurity 102
4. Tables 108

Notes 117

References 127

Index 135

Illustrations

1. Bengali terms for kinsmen (male ego) 10

2. Bengali terms for kinsmen (married female ego) 11

3. Relationship between *jñāti* and *kuṭumba* classes 16

4. Schematic outline of the structure of Bengali Hindu marriage 53

Acknowledgments

The collaboration represented in this book began as long ago as 1959 when we were both students of the Bengali language under Edward C. Dimock, Jr., to whom we owe a special debt for all the research on Bengal we have since done. We took up the analysis of Bengali kinship in 1970 at the Asian Studies Center at Michigan State University, and we express our warm gratitude to its director, William T. Ross, for the facilities and encouragement he provided. The manuscript was completed at the University of Chicago, where the Lichtstern Research Fund of the Department of Anthropology and the Committee on Southern Asian Studies provided the infrastructure for our work.

We presented the first version of this analysis to the 1970 Annual Conference on Bengal Studies held at Oakland University. Anyone interested in seeing the number and variety of mistakes that can be made in an analysis of this kind may read that paper in *Prelude to Crisis: Bengal and Bengal Studies in 1970*, edited by Peter J. Bertocci (East Lansing: Asian Studies Center, South Asia Occasional Paper no. 18, 1972). A more advanced version of the analysis was prepared for the conference on Kinship and History in South Asia organized by Thomas R. Trautmann and Narendra K. Wagle and held at the University of Toronto. The proceedings of this fruitful conference were published, edited by Trautmann (Ann Arbor: Michigan Papers on South and Southeast Asia, no. 7, 1974), but our contribution was not included there since it was already too long to be regarded as a paper. The conference discussions provided us with important stimulation.

Since neither of us is a Bengali, we have made many mistakes in our attempts to understand Bengali culture, and time and again our Bengali friends have patiently explained our errors to us. Foremost among these is Tarasish Mukhopadhyay, an anthropologist who has worked with both of us in the field in rural Bengal. During several years they spent in Chicago, Shamsul Bari, Pabitra Bhusan Sarkar, and Aditi Nath Sarkar were invaluable consultants on many topics.

Our colleagues in the field of Bengal studies have been generous with both information and criticism as we worked out this analysis. We would like to thank Mary Higdon Beech, Peter J. Bertocci, Jean Ellickson, Akos Ostor, Lina Fruzzetti, and Manisha Roy for helping and challenging us.

Lengthy (and often heated) interchanges with a number of scholars have helped us clarify our argument. We thank André Béteille, Anthony Carter, Bernard S. Cohn, Kenneth David, Ranajit Guha, Suzanne Hanchett, Carl Pletsch, A. K. Ramanujan, William B. Sewell, A. M. Shah, Henri Stern, Patricia Uberoi, and Sylvia Vatuk. In addition, the students in our course on Kinship and Marriage in South Asia have provided us with many hours of stimulating discussion on these topics.

Harold Scheffler gave us the benefit of a painstaking criticism of an earlier version of the manuscript from the perspective of an anthropological kinship specialist. Thomas Trautmann did so from the perspective of a historian of ancient India and a student of Indian systems of kinship and marriage. Our greatest intellectual debt is to David M. Schneider, whose study *American Kinship* provided the initial conception of this book, and who also commented extensively on the manuscript.

It is not possible here to thank all of our Bengali friends in Calcutta, Dacca, and the villages in which we have lived. Hundreds of people gave freely of their time to discuss with us the matters we consider here, and thousands of others helped unwittingly simply by being themselves and observing the precepts of their culture while we looked on. Since we cannot thank all these people individually, we have dedicated the book to them.

Both of us were supported by the Foreign Area Fellowship Program (then known as Ford Foundation Foreign Area Training Fellowships) when we first did research in Bengal—Nicholas in 1960–61 and Inden in 1963–64. A Fulbright-Hays Senior Research Fellowship and a grant from the Office of International Studies and Programs at Michigan State University supported additional field research in 1968–69 and 1970 by Nicholas. A fellowship from the National Endowment for the Humanities made possible additional archival research in England by Inden. Amy Arnett Knoespel typed the final manuscript with great care and a keen eye for inconsistencies; Susan Hopkins prepared the illustrations.

Introduction

Bengal is a cultural and linguistic region on the eastern extremity of the South Asian subcontinent, with the hills of Burma on its southeastern border. The region is defined by its predominant language, Bengali, which belongs to the Indo-European family and is descended from Sanskrit. A distinctive Bengali literary tradition can be traced to about the fourteenth century. The cultural region of Bengal includes both the independent nation of Bangladesh and the state of West Bengal in India. Together these two territories have a population of more than 125 million persons, the great majority of whom consider themselves Bengalis.

Although the region is relatively compact and much of it is characterized by a uniform deltaic terrain, there are notable subregional differences of dialect, settlement pattern, customary social practices, and so forth. Moreover, the Bengalis themselves perceive great differences of society and culture between the metropolis of Calcutta or the Bangladesh capital, Dacca, on the one hand, and the "rustic" countryside on the other. Despite this diversity, however, Bengalis commonly speak of a single "Bengali society" (Vaṅger *samāja*) and "Bengali culture" (Vaṅger *saṃskṛti*). In undertaking this study of kinship in Bengali culture we have accepted the Bengali idea that there is, at some level of generality, a Bengali culture.

The most obvious division in Bengali society and culture arises from the difference between Muslims and Hindus, between Islam as a religion and what has come to be called "the Hindu religion" (*Hindu dharma*). Hindus constitute a majority of the population in West Bengal; Muslims are a majority in Bangladesh and among all Bengalis. The research that each of us has done over the past fifteen years or so has made us more familiar with Bengali Hindu culture than with that of Bengali Muslims. Therefore, most of what we say here about Bengali culture should be understood to apply to Bengali Hindu culture. There is much in common between Hindu and Muslim culture in Bengal, but many of the relationships and activities we discuss, for example, the *saṃskāra* ("life cycle") rites, are distinctively Hindu. (Some of these distinctions are discussed in Appendix 2.) In a similar way, much of what we here speak of as "Bengali kinship" appears to be shared with other regions of South Asia. Our preliminary comparisons with other anthropological accounts of kinship in India have shown that categories of kinship in North India, if not also in the South, are structured in much the same way as the Bengali categories. That this is so is also confirmed by data derived from textual accounts of Indian kinship. Much of what we say about kinship in Bengali Hindu culture is derived from ancient and medieval Sanskrit texts; Bengali Hindus share these with Hindus throughout South Asia, implying the existence of an all-Indian "culture of kinship." It is somewhat surprising, however, to find little discrepancy between the categories and symbols of kinship in the literary tradition of Hinduism and those of the regional traditions represented in anthropological accounts.

At a superficial level there is much variation, even within Bengal, in the specific content of relations among "kinsmen" according to their caste, locality, and religious orientation. Moreover, there are distinctions between urban and rural Bengalis that often correlate closely with the differences between educated and uneducated persons. Yet we are convinced that a single coherent pattern of symbols, which we have abstracted from very diverse materials, underlies most of the specific variant forms. This is not to say that "the Bengali kinship system" has not changed or is not changing, but rather that this pattern comprehends most of what we have learned from "modern" Bengalis (some of whom profess not to be practicing Hindus) as well as what we have learned from "ordinary" villagers and from "ancient" literary sources. The problems of variation and change are authentic but will have to wait for later work.

Culture and Symbolism

The approach we have taken to the category of "kinship" in Bengali culture is derived primarily from that of David M. Schneider in his analysis, *American Kinship* (1968). With Schneider, we regard a "kinship system" as a cultural system. By a cultural system we mean a *system of symbols* or, to be more precise, a system of *meanings* of symbols. We do not say very much about social relations among "kinsmen" in Bengali society; rather, we examine the symbols of

Bengali culture that have meanings connected with social solidarity, whether in the form of "duties" (*kartavya*) or in one of the many differentiated forms of "love" (*prema*). We seek to understand how these symbols are connected and how Bengalis use them to define relationships. It may appear that such a culturally specific approach makes comparisons with kinship systems in other cultures impossible—that we have adopted an extreme position of cultural relativism. This is not the case: symbols and their use can be compared across cultural boundaries as precisely as can, for example, frequencies of family types, lineage composition, or birthrates. We hope to demonstrate this with some comparative remarks in the course of this analysis.

We use the term "symbol" in its most general sense to refer, in Schneider's words (1968, p. 1), to "something which stands for something else, or some things else, where there is no necessary or intrinsic relationship between the symbol and that which it symbolizes." The symbols—or meanings—that belong to any cultural domain may be said to constitute a system only insofar as the persons who share those meanings connect them to one another. Thus, if there is a Bengali "kinship system," it includes *only* those symbols defined by Bengali culture as belonging to the domain of "kinship," and it includes all such symbols.

Fundamental to Schneider's approach is the theoretical distinction between the cultural system of a society and the total social system to which it is connected. A cultural system, according to Schneider (1968, p. 1), is "a system of units (or parts) which are defined in certain ways and which are differentiated according to certain criteria. These units define the world or the universe, the way things in it relate to each other, and what these things should be and do." Schneider defines and differentiates the units or parts of the American cultural system by reference to their "distinctive" or "defining features," a concept borrowed from linguistics. He found that two symbolic features, operating either singly or in combination, define the domain of kinship in American culture—shared "blood," an inherited *natural* substance, and "love," a particular *moral* code for conduct. Shared or inherited "substance" (*dhātu*) and "code for conduct" (*dharma*) prove also to be the two features by which kinship is defined in Bengali culture. However, there is a fundamental difference between the ways in which Americans and Bengalis connect these two features.

Kinship, for Bengali Hindus, is premised upon the cultural assumption that all beings are organized into *jāti*, genera (see Marriott and Inden 1974, pp. 983–84). The term *jāti* is often properly translated as "caste," but in Bengali it is used to refer to a number of smaller genera as well. A person is thought to be born into a particular clan (*kula*), family (*parivāra*), and sex (*strī-jāti*, "female genus," or *puruṣa-jāti*, "male genus"). Each genus is defined by its particular substance and code, which are thought to be inseparable from one another. Thus the code for conduct of a particular clan, family, or sex is thought to be imbedded in the bodily substance shared by the persons of each genus and to be inherited by birth. As a consequence of this cultural premise, no distinction is made, as in American culture, between an order of "nature," defined by shared biogenetic substance, and an order of "law," defined by code for conduct. Similarly, no distinction is made between a "material" or "secular" order and a "spiritual" or "sacred" order. Thus, in Bengali culture there is a single order of beings, an order that in Western terms is both natural and moral, both material and spiritual.

Parallel to the inseparable relationship of code and substance in Bengali culture is a conception of the relationship between "symbol" and "referent." The concept of "symbol" is primarily employed by the analyst. However, in Euro-American societies such concepts as "symbol" and "metaphor" may be used in ordinary discourse. Thus, persons usually think of a wedding ring as an arbitrary symbol of marriage and of the expression "one flesh" as a "material" metaphor for the "spiritual" unity of husband and wife. Comparable symbols in Bengali Hindu culture are not commonly perceived to have "arbitrary" or "conventional" relations to their referents. For instance, the streak of red color worn in the parting of the hair of a Bengali Hindu married woman whose husband is alive is said to be homologous with her uterine blood, her contribution to the procreation of a child. Similarly, when a man speaks of his wife as his "half-body" he is not saying that she is "like" his half-body but rather that she *is* his half-body, made into his substance by marriage.

Symbols are often thought of as "things"—whether words, laws, persons, flags, emblems, totems, or whatever. However, the concept of symbol we use in this book also includes actions. The persons who share a cultural system do not regard all symbolic things as equally important: a house in a particular neighborhood may be a "status symbol," valued by many, but it is not of the same importance or centrality to all as a cross or a national flag. So, too, some symbolic actions are more central than others to particular cultural systems. Such central symbolic acts are typically laden with a greater than usual variety of meanings—they are "multivocal" or "polysemic" (see Turner 1967, pp. 27–32; 1969, pp. 8–14)—and they constitute paradigms for other kinds of symbolic action.

Here we are concerned with three classes of central symbolic actions. First, there are symbolic acts that create the solidary units of a society in their totality. In our own culture, marriage is such a symbolic act, one that creates a new family. Blood covenants and sacrifices are examples of symbolic acts said to create communities of believers. Social compacts and constitutions are examples of "secular" symbolic acts that are thought to create nations or bodies politic. Second, new "members" are "incorporated" into these solidary units through symbolic acts of initiation such as baptism or christening, first communion, oaths of allegiance, ordination, coronation, and naturalization. A third kind of symbolic act of concern to us is that which recreates, restores, reiterates, or reinvigorates a set of solidary relationships. Often tied to a calendar, such actions include the eucharist, the daily pledge to a flag, the recitation of a creed, the family meal, "making love," and quadrennial elections.

While the relationship between a symbolic *thing* and its referents may be considered "arbitrary" by the persons of a given society, the relationship between the type of symbolic *action* and referent enumerated above is rarely treated as such. People frequently regard the relationship between these central symbolic acts and their referents to be one of cause and effect. For example, in Christianity, baptism is sometimes spoken of as an "efficient symbol" because it not only signifies the removal from a child of its original sin but also accomplishes that cleansing. The central symbolic actions in Bengali culture are thought of, in very much the same way, as both symbolizing and, if properly done, achieving their objectives.

Among the most important things used as symbols in Bengali culture are a person's body (*śarīra*), his house (*gṛha*), food (*anna*), semen (*śukra*) or "seed" (*bīja*), the womb (*garbha*) or "field" (*kṣetra*), appropriate codes for conduct (*dharma*), love (*prema*), and purity (*śauca*) and its opposite, impurity (*aśauca*). However, these symbolic things do not stand alone but are more often than not seen by Bengalis in contexts of symbolic action. Among the most important of the central symbolic actions with which we deal here are the *saṃskāra* rites. Some *saṃskāra*s, such as marriage (*vivāha*), create new solidary units (although the Bengali marriage, unlike its Euro-American counterpart, is not thought to break up old families). Other *saṃskāra*s, such as initiation (*upanayana* or *dīkṣā*), recruit persons to solidary units. Some of them both create solidary units and initiate persons into them; all of them may serve the purpose of reinvigorating or reiterating existing relationships.

About This Research

Although we cannot claim to have freed ourselves from all the preconceptions of American culture concerning what "kinship" is and how a "kinsman" is defined, we have attempted to be consistent in interposing Bengali categories and symbols between our data and our analysis. Previous students of North Indian kinship have generally assumed the existence of some universal scientific categories, such as "family" ("nuclear" and "joint"), "consanguines" (especially "agnates" in North India), "cognates," and "affines." They have assumed that a person's "real" kinsmen could be diagrammed on a chart showing genealogical and marriage connections and that persons "treated as" kinsmen, whose relationships could not be shown on such a chart, were "fictive" kin. "Clans," and later "lineages," were found among other "corporate kinship groups" in South Asia, as elsewhere in the world. In the past, we too have assumed the existence of such categories. It was largely the discomfort we felt in describing Bengali families as "patrilocal" and "patrilineally extended" or in asserting that Bengalis belong to "bilateral, ego-centered kin groups" that impelled us to undertake this analysis. In short, the assumptions that have been made in the study of North Indian kinship systems have led to a great deal of confusion. We think that approaching Bengali kinship through the categories and assumptions of Bengali culture itself diminishes confusion and provides a parsimonious account of relations among kinsmen in Bengal.

One of us (Nicholas) is an anthropologist and the other (Inden) a historian. Nicholas began his work in Bengal in 1960–61 with a study of the ecology of rural settlement in deltaic West Bengal. Inden went to Bengal in 1963–64 to do a historical study of marriage and rank among the highest Hindu castes. Both of these projects yielded, as almost incidental products, several hundred genealogies. In 1968–69 and 1970 Nicholas returned to West Bengal for a study of the symbolism of Hindu rituals. During the course of village census work at that time he collected several hundred additional genealogies as well as a greatly deepened working understanding of kinship in Bengali culture. Although Inden is a historian who works primarily in ancient and medieval Sanskrit and Bengali texts, he also did fieldwork among very low-caste as well as among high-caste people. Although Nicholas is an anthropologist who works primarily through interviews and observations in the villages, he has worked with medieval Bengali texts. Both of us have spent some time among Muslim Bengalis in Bangladesh and among urban Bengalis in Calcutta, the great metropolis of Bengal, which turns out to be less different from the countryside than we might have imagined.

Neither of us undertook a special study of kinship in Bengal, but in 1970, as we began to discuss major problems in the study of Bengali society, it became apparent to us that this was a necessary preliminary to much of what we wished to say about ritual symbolism, religion in general, and the whole social order as Bengalis see it. On the basis of our experience in and continuous work on Bengali culture, we were intuitively convinced that Bengali kinship usages fell into a highly structured pattern. However, neither the structural-functional nor the structuralist methods generally employed in the analysis of kinship systems revealed more than a partial pattern, and they left many awkward problems dangling. Even after we undertook to deal with Bengali kinship in the terms provided by Bengali culture, as Schneider had done for American kinship, we still made many mistakes, most of which our Bengali friends have patiently corrected for us, though no doubt some errors still remain. The first chapter presents the structure of Bengali kinship categories and explains why they are structured this way according to Bengalis. Chapter 2 examines the "life cycle rites" (*saṃskāra*s), the symbolic acts through which kin relationships are created and transformed. Finally, we examine the ways in which Bengali "kinship terminology" is related to the structure and transformation of kin relationships.

Kinship in Bengali Culture

1 *Ātmīya-svajana:* One's Own People

Classes of "Kin"

The Bengali compound term *ātmīya-svajana* is very commonly used in contexts where the Western observer seems obliged to gloss it as "relatives," "kinsmen," or perhaps "kith and kin." For example, when Bengalis are asked whom they invited to a daughter's marriage, they commonly reply "our *ātmīya-svajana*." Or when asked what relationship (*samparka*) they have with persons who live in a neighboring house, villagers often say, "they are our *ātmīya-svajana*." The term *ātmīya* comes from the reflexive word *ātma* and means "one's own"; the term *svajana* means "one's" (*sva-*) "people" (*-jana*). Both terms combined together are used in Bengali to designate "one's own people." At the outset of our inquiry we thought that the two words which make up this compound term would refer to two distinct and complementary classes of one's own people. We soon found that this was not so. Used alone, each of these terms may refer to a single person; combined, however, they refer to one's own people in the plural.

When asked to provide a definition of "one's own people," Bengalis commonly told us that they were persons related by "blood" (*rakta*) or by the "same body" (*eka-śarīra, sapiṇḍa*). At the same time they also said that some persons not related by shared bodily substance are also "one's own people": persons related by marriage, by living together in the same house, neighborhood, or village, by being members of the same school class, by working together in the same office, by taking instruction from the same *guru*, by going on pilgrimage together, and so forth. It seemed significant, and at the same time was maddening, that almost every informant gave a list such as this and ended it with "and so forth." In fact, when pressed, several informants explicitly stated that almost anyone could, under appropriate circumstances, be considered "one's own person." Our personal experiences in Bengal have more than confirmed this view: each of us is "elder brother," "mother's brother," "father's younger brother," and so on, to innumerable persons, not only in villages but also in some of the most "modern" parts of Calcutta.

While the words *ātmīya* and *svajana* are compounded in Bengali and used in an undifferentiated way to designate an open set of people, two different words—*jñāti* and *kuṭumba*—are used in a quite different sense. The compounded form of these two words, *jñāti-kuṭumba*, is, like *ātmīya-svajana*, used to refer to "one's own people," but in a more restricted sense. Almost anyone can be designated as *ātmīya-svajana*, but only some of one's own people can be designated as *jñāti-kuṭumba*, and the same persons are invariably so designated. The term *jñāti-kuṭumba*[1] thus refers to a definite, closed subset of one's own people.

Kula and *Parivāra*: Clan and Family

Bengalis classify their own people not only as *ātmīya-svajana* and *jñāti-kuṭumba* but also as persons of particular solidary units referred to by such terms as *kula* and *parivāra*. The terms *ātmīya-svajana* and *jñāti-kuṭumba* are used by a man to refer to sets of persons related to him in a variety of ways; they are "ego-centered" and do not designate solidary units. The terms *kula* and *parivāra*, by contrast, are used to refer to sets of persons related to one another in a particular way; they are not ego-centered and they do designate solidary units.

The term *kula* refers to a set of one's own people, taking a "seed male" or "ancestral male" (*bīja-puruṣa, pūrva-puruṣa*) and not "ego" as its referent. A number of other terms, such as *vaṃśa, goṣṭhī*, and *gotra*, are often used interchangeably with *kula*, although each of these is also used to designate units similar to but different from the *kula*. *Kula* designates a unit often referred to as a "patrilineage" or, less commonly, a "clan." It includes persons related to a common *dead* ancestral male; that is, a *kula* includes all of the male descendants of a common ancestral male, together with their wives and unmarried daughters. Persons who belong to the same *kula* are referred to as *sagotra* or *sakulya* (which also has a more restricted meaning, see p. 15). One's own people who belong to different *kula*s are referred to as *asagotra* or *bhinna-gotra* ("different *gotra*"). Similarly modified forms of the term *kula* are used to distinguish persons of different *kulas: pitṛ-kula*, father's *kula; mātṛ-kula*, mother's father's *kula*; *svāmī-kula,* husband's *kula*, and so forth.

A *gotra* is a clanlike unit defined not by shared bodily substance but by a shared name, the personal name of an original Brahman priest-preceptor (*ṛṣi*). All persons who share the same *gotra* name are said to be of the same *gotra*, regardless of differences of *kula* or caste. The *gotra* names of Brahmans were originally obtained in the same way as their bodily substance: the *gotra* ancestor of a Brahman was also the ancestral male of the particular ancestral male of his *kula*. Non-Brahmans, however, originally acquired their *gotra* names from their *kula* priests (*kula-purohita*). *Gotra* is not so important in the definition of a solidary social unit as it is in worship.

The term *gotra* refers to a name; the term *vaṃśa*, which also means "bamboo," refers to the particular bodily substance of males (their semen). In its most common usage, *vaṃśa* is a synonym for the term *kula*. However, in a more restricted sense it means "children" or "offspring" (*santāna-santati*), and particularly a male child. Like a bamboo, which is a series of continuously linked and growing nodes, the *vaṃśa* par excellence is the continuing succession of males (*puruṣa-paramparā*) in a *kula*, excluding its outmarrying daughters and inmarrying wives.

The term *parivāra* refers to a set of one's own people taking a *living* rather than a dead male as its referent. This set of persons, a subset of the *kula*, is often referred to as a "family" of one kind or another. It includes persons related by shared bodily substance to a common living man called a *svāmī* or "master": his wife, his sons, his sons' wives and sons, and perhaps even their wives and sons. The unmarried daughters of these men are included only temporarily. It is stated quite explicitly that a married daughter belongs not to her father's *parivāra* but to her husband's.

Parivāra means "dependent" of a master. The first and foremost dependent of a man is his wife, and the term *parivāra* may be used to refer to his wife alone. However, a wife (*strī*) alone is not regarded as the "minimal" family necessary for a man. In order to perpetuate the *kula*, he should be the father (*bābā*) and genitor (*janaka*) and his wife the mother (*mā*) and genetrix (*jananī*) of at least one son (*chele*); his family may also include their other sons and daughters (*meye*), who are brothers (*bhāi*) and sisters (*bon*) to one another. This set of eight relationships is regarded as encompassing the closest bodily relationships among one's own people, and the terms that designate these eight classes of persons are clearly distinguished from the terms for other relatives, as we shall show in chapter 3.

The unit comprising this set of relationships—a married couple and their unmarried children—appears to be identical with the "nuclear," "conjugal," or "elementary" family of sociology. From a purely "compositional" standpoint this is so. However, it is usually assumed in studies of the family that such a unit constitutes a culturally bounded and complete set, clearly demarcated from another kind of unit comprising more than one married couple and designated as a "joint" or "extended" family. The difficulty with respect to the Bengali Hindu family is that such a "nuclear" unit is not a culturally closed set. In fact, while a man need have only a wife and one son, if he "gives birth" (as a Bengali man may do) to daughters or to more than one son, these too automatically become his dependents or family. This process of including additional dependents may go on indefinitely: the wives of a man's sons become dependents of their masters (husbands), and so do the children. However, these added sets of masters and dependents do not form distinct families, since their respective masters are themselves dependents of their father and master so long as he remains alive.

Bengalis do not regard a family made up of a man, his wife, and their children—what we refer to as a "minimal family"—and a family made up of a man, his wife, their sons, son's wives, and children, and so on—what we call a "maximal family"—as being two contrasting and opposed types. All the persons related by sharing the body of the same living master, no matter how many "lineally" or "collaterally" related males there may be, constitute his *parivāra-varga*, the aggregate of his bodily dependents. The open-ended and continuously incorporating character of this unit is reflected in the way Bengalis define "membership" in the family in the written language, where a man's family (*parivāra*) is referred to as including *strī-putrādi*. This compound term is best defined as "the set of those persons having the wife and son as its first (and foremost) members."

Each of the married men in such a unit is designated a *svāmī*, "master" in relation to his dependent wife and children. But only one man is master of the entire incorporating set in its totality. This master, the living man whose body all others share, is distinguished from the other masters as their *kartā*. Derived from the root *kṛ*, meaning "act," "make," "perform," "manage," the word *kartā* literally means "actor," "he who independently performs enjoined actions for his house (*gṛha*) and his bodily dependents (*parivāra-varga*)." By far the most important symbolic actions performed by the *kartā* or *svāmī* are acts of worship; in fact, the major "role" played by a man as master is that of "sacrificer" (*yajamāna*).

The distinction between a man's "family" and his "house" or "household" (*gṛha, bāṛi*) lies in the fact that the house is a place (*sthāna*). Persons who live together in the same house are considered to form a solidary unit. However, their relationship is defined not by shared bodily substance but by sharing a house. This distinction may seem inconsequential since, almost invariably, it is the persons of one family who share a house. However, Bengalis make use of this distinction. The only person who may speak of his dependents is a master; thus, not every person can refer to "my family" (*āmār parivāra*), but only the man who is its master. The persons of his family, who share in his body, may refer to him as "our master" (*āmāder kartā*). So, too, the persons who share a house may speak of "our house" (*āmāder bāṛi*) and of the "persons of our house" (*āmāder bāṛir lok*). In the contexts where an English-speaker might refer to "his family" a Bengali may refer to "the people of his house."[2] Since the house is not defined by shared bodily substance, it may, under certain circumstances, include persons not related to its master (*gṛhastha, gṛha-kartā*, or *bāṛir mālik*) by shared bodily substance, such as servants.

There is considerable confusion in the literature on joint families in India, in part because of the failure to distinguish between the shared body relationship and the sharing of a house. It is often the case that persons of a man's family appear not to live in his house. Aside from short-term absences, a man's son, and that son's wife and children, may dwell in another neighborhood, another town or village, or even another country. This need not mean, however, that "nuclearization" of the family has taken place. For as long as his father is alive, he and his family are considered to be part of his father's family, and the place where they reside is not their house (*bāṛi*) but their "nest" (*bāsā*).

Conversely, a number of related married couples and their children, and so forth, may share the same house without constituting a family. The house may consist of anything from a multistory, labyrinthine unitary structure, such as is found in north Calcutta, to a series of discrete mud and bamboo huts clustered together on a plot of raised land in a deltaic village; each is equally a "house" according to Bengalis. Such a house may contain upward of a hundred people. The core of this unit consists of a number of men, each the master of his own family, who together share the body of a common ancestral male. They do not, however, share the body of a common living male. Hence, such a unit consists not of one master and his family but of a number of masters and their families. Mastery among these men is graded first according to generation, then according to order of birth. The senior master may be referred to as *baṛo kartā*, the second as *mejo kartā*, and so on in a series (for a discussion of these seniority terms see p. 73). Such a unit may be referred to in Bengali as a *goṣṭhī*; anthropologists would refer to it as a "localized patrilineage" or a "localized descent group." While the term *goṣṭhī* may be used by Hindus synonymously with *kula*, the two terms denote different solidary units (for the Muslim usage of *goṣṭhī* see Appendix 2). All persons who share the body of the same ancestral male, whether they live together or not, belong to the same *kula*, but only those persons of a *kula* who share the same house belong to a *goṣṭhī*.

Finally, both the *kula* and *goṣṭhī* are culturally differentiated from the *parivāra* or family itself. Persons who share the body of a common living male belong to the same *parivāra*. Since it is normally presumed that persons of the same family also share the same house, a *parivāra* may be equated with a "house" or "household" but, as we have seen, it need not be. For the sake of convenience where it seems necessary, we shall translate *parivāra* as "family" and *kula* as "clan." It should be understood, however, that neither of the Bengali terms means what is normally meant in English by "family" or "clan."

The *Jñāti* Class of One's Own People

The compound term *jñāti-kuṭumba* refers not to clans and families, but rather to the set of one's own people, taking ego as the referent. Unlike the *ātmīya-svajana* category, this ego-centered set of kinsmen has definite limits. The terms *jñāti* and *kuṭumba* are used to refer to two opposed but overlapping sets of kinsmen. The *jñāti* set is similar to the category of "blood" relatives in American kinship and the "cognatic kindred" or "consanguine" categories of anthropology, but it is not the same as any of these categories. Likewise, the *kuṭumba* set is similar to the category of relatives "by marriage" or "in-law" in American kinship—the anthropologist's "affines"—but it is not the same.

The word *jñāti* is used in both an unrestricted and a restricted, par excellence, sense. We will use the word *jñāti* by itself to denote the inclusive, unrestricted sense of that term. We will refer to the restricted set of *jñāti*—a set resembling the "agnates" of anthropological analysis—as "par excellence *jñāti*." Since the set of *jñāti* opposed to this restricted set is not designated by a generic term in Bengali, we shall refer to it as the "residual *jñāti*," even though, in certain contexts, persons belonging to this so-called residual class may be considered more important than persons belonging to the par excellence class. The residual *jñāti* class is similar to the "cognates" of kinship studies.

The set of par excellence *jñāti* includes the men, unmarried women, and inmarrying women of "one's own clan" (*nijer kula*). For a man, whether married or unmarried, his own clan is his father's clan (*pitṛ-kula*).[3] His set of par excellence *jñāti* includes men such as his father, father's father, father's father's father, father's brothers, father's brothers' sons, brothers, sons, father's brothers' sons' sons, and the like; unmarried women such as his sisters, father's brothers' daughters, his own and his brothers' daughters, and so on; and inmarrying women such as his wife, mother, father's mother, father's father's mother, father's brothers' wives, father's brothers' sons' wives, brothers' wives, brothers' sons' wives, sons' wives, and so forth. Figure 1 illustrates the classification of par excellence *jñāti* for a man in a genealogical format. For a woman, however, there is a difference. Before marriage her own clan is her father's clan; after marriage her own clan is her husband's clan (*pati-kula*). Thus, the set of par excellence *jñāti* for a married woman is identical with that of her husband. His par excellence *jñāti*, the men, unmarried women, and inmarrying women of his clan, also constitute her par excellence *jñāti*. Figure 2 illustrates the classification of par excellence *jñāti* for a married woman in a genealogical format. When Bengalis use the term *jñāti*, they most commonly use it in the restricted sense to denote the par excellence set of *jñāti*.

The other, opposed set of *jñāti*, the "residual" set, includes both the persons of one's mother's father's clan (*mātṛ-kula*) and the outmarrying women from one's own clan together with their children.[4] His set of "residual" *jñāti* includes men of his *mātṛ-kula*, such as

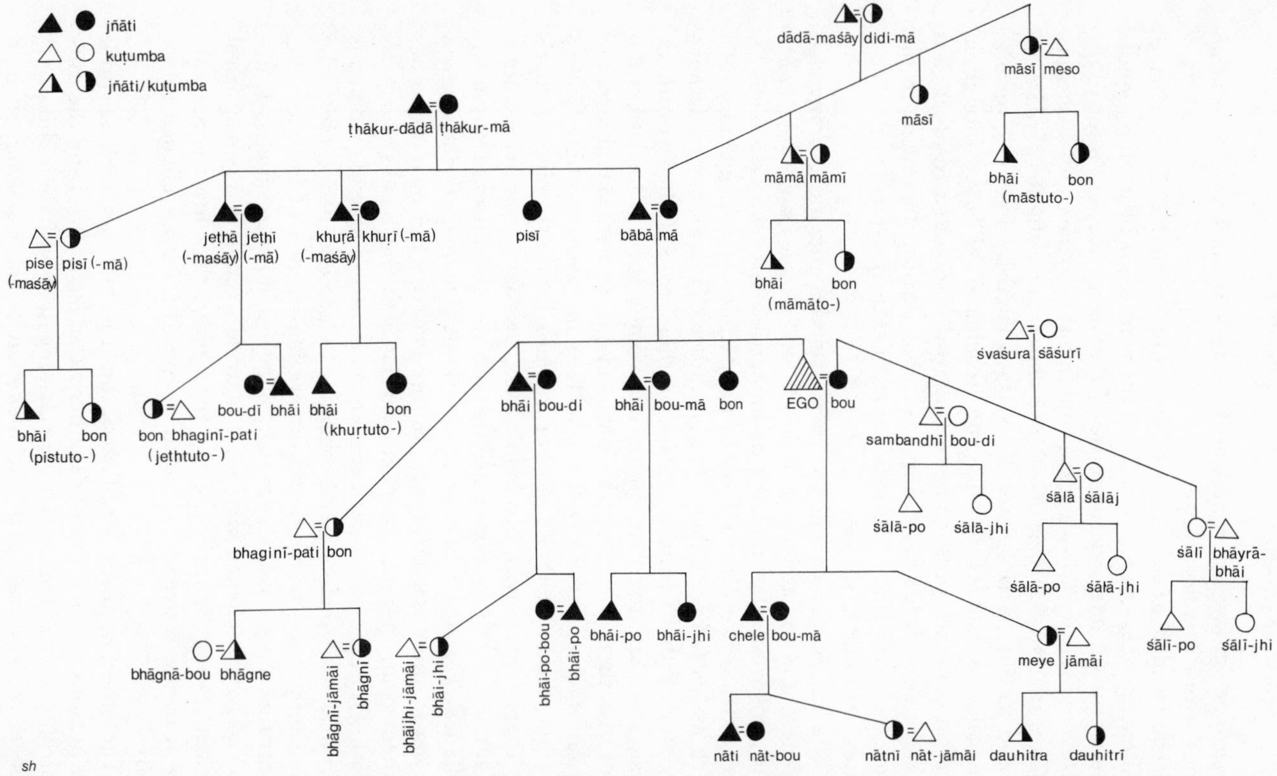

Fig. 1. Bengali terms for kinsmen (male ego)

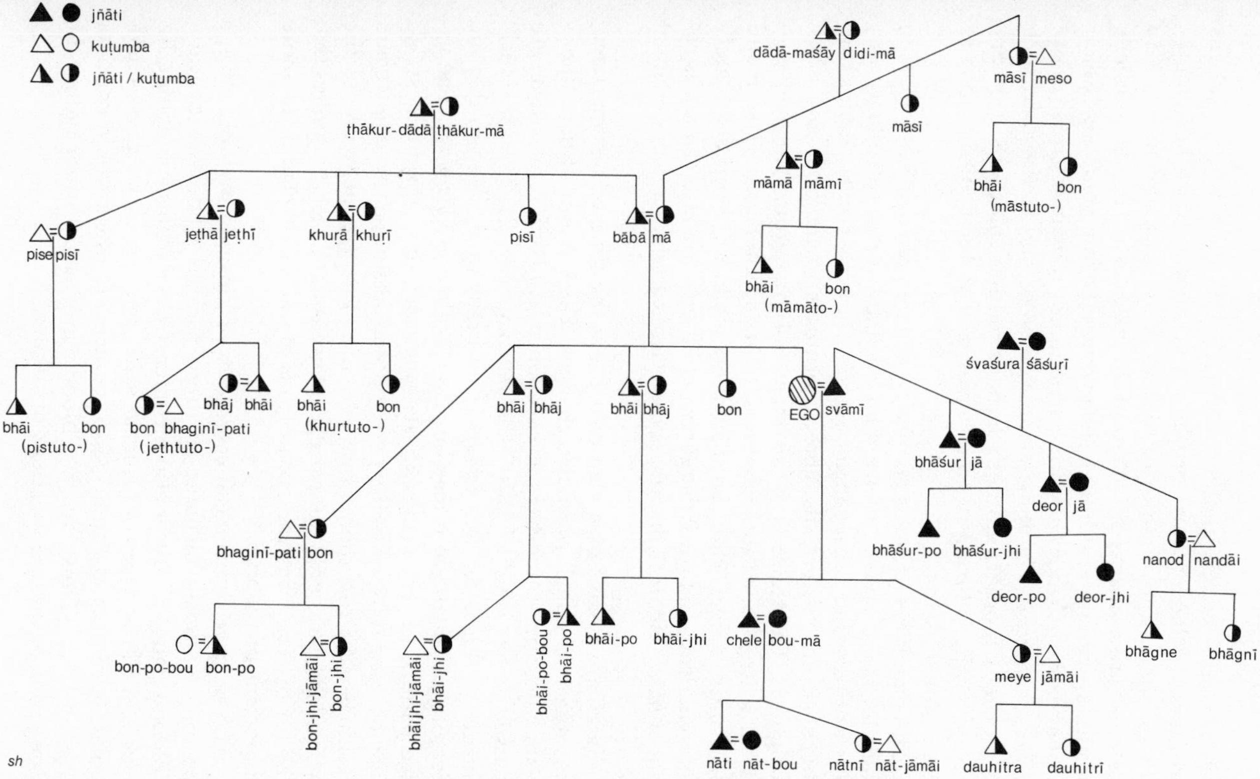

Fig. 2. Bengali terms for kinsmen (married female ego)

his mother's father, mother's father's father, mother's father's brothers, mother's father's brothers' sons, mother's brothers, mother's brothers' sons, mother's brothers' sons' sons, and so on. Also included are unmarried women of the *mātṛ-kula*, such as mother's brothers' daughters; although such women become persons of their husbands' *kula*s when they are married, they remain in one's residual *jñāti* category. The inmarrying women of one's *mātṛ-kula*, such as mother's mother, mother's father's mother, mother's brothers' wives, mother's brothers' sons' wives, and so forth, also belong to the residual *jñāti*.

The daughters of one's *pitṛ-kula* become par excellence *jñāti* in their husbands' *kula*s and are then classified as one's residual *jñāti*; this outmarrying subset includes one's father's sisters, father's father's sisters, sisters, daughters, brothers' daughters, and sons' daughters. The children of the women of the outmarrying subset—father's sisters' sons and daughters, father's father's sisters' sons and daughters, sisters' children, daughters' children, brothers' daughters' children, and sons' daughters' children—are also classed as residual *jñāti*. Figure 1 illustrates the classification of a man's residual *jñāti*.

Since a woman's own clan changes at the time of her marriage, her set of "residual" *jñāti* also changes. The persons of her father's clan, who constituted her par excellence *jñāti* before marriage, are classed as her residual *jñāti* after marriage (fig. 2). The "residual" quality of this latter set of *jñāti* is culturally recognized in that the persons belonging to it may be also classified as *kuṭumba*s. The usage pattern of the term *jñāti* also indicates this "residualness." It may be used to refer to the two opposed sets of par excellence and residual *jñāti* together. However, the more frequent use of the word designates only the par excellence set and clearly implies that the set of *jñāti* consisting of persons of one's own clan is the more important of the two.

To compare the Bengali categories of kinsmen with our own, a person's *jñāti* set includes all those persons whom we consider "blood relatives." But it also includes, from a man's standpoint, his wife and all the wives of his male *jñāti*, and, from a woman's standpoint, her husband and his *jñāti*, people whom we would consider her "in-laws." Thus, clearly, "blood" and "law" do not define the categories of kinsmen in Bengali culture.

What then are the defining features of the *jñāti* set of kinsmen? The term *jñāti* is synonymous with the terms *eka-deha, eka-śarīra*, and most important, *sapiṇḍa*. Like the term *jñāti*, the term *sapiṇḍa* is used in an unrestricted and a restricted sense to include more and less comprehensive sets of persons. Each of these terms means "sharing the same body" and provides one feature that defines the *jñāti* class of "one's own people." The most succinct and famous definition of the *sapiṇḍa* relationship as a shared body relationship occurs in Vijñāneśvara's Mitākṣarā, a commentary written around A.D. 1100 on the influential code book of Yājñavalkya, compiled by a school of *śāstra* scholars between A.D. 100 and 300:

> The shared body relationship [*sapiṇḍatā*] comes about by virtue of connection [*anvaya*] with portions [*avayava*] of the same body [*eka-śarīra*]. Thus, by virtue of connection with portions of the father's body, the son comes to have a shared body relationship with the father and through the father with the set of those beginning with the father's father as well, because of the connection with portions of his body. Similarly, by virtue of connection with portions of the mother's body he comes to have a shared body relationship with the mother and through the mother with the set of those beginning with the mother's father. Likewise, there is a shared body relationship both with the mother's sisters and mother's brothers and with the father's brothers and father's sisters by virtue of connection with portions of the same body. So, too, the wife comes to have a shared body relationship with the husband by virtue of their reproduction of the same body [*eka-śarīrārambhakatayā*]. Similarly, the wives of brothers also come to have a shared body relationship, the one with the other [*paraspara*], because they have the relationship of reproducing the same body with those men reproduced from the same body. Thus, wherever the word *sapiṇḍa* occurs it is to be understood as connection with portions of the same body either direct [*sākṣāt*] or by succession [*paramparayā*].[5]

The class of persons designated here by Vijñāneśvara as sharing the same body is clearly identical in content to that demarcated by the term *jñāti* in its unrestricted Bengali usage, encompassing not only par excellence *jñāti*, persons of the father's *kula*, but also residual *jñāti*, persons of the mother's *kula* as well. More significant is the inclusion of a man's wife and the wives of his brothers. Their inclusion in the set of shared body relationships contrasts strongly with the categorization of consanguines and affines in Euro-American culture. We shall return to a discussion of this important issue when we take up marriage (chap. 2).

Another term, *dharma*, is regularly associated with the terms *jñāti* and *kula*. The word *dharma* is derived from the Sanskrit root *dhṛ* meaning "to support, uphold, or sustain." According to the authoritative Bengali dictionary of J. M. Dāsa (1937), *dharma* is that which "sustains" (*dhāraṇa*) or "nourishes" (*poṣaṇa*) everything. In particular, *dharma* refers to those actions (*karma*) which are to be done (*kartavya*)—to that conduct (*ācāra*) which is enjoined (*vihita*) and good (*sat*)—foremost among which is worshiping the gods: in other words, the "code for conduct" by which a set of people is sustained and nourished. Differently defined sets of people have different codes for conduct. *Jñāti-dharma* is the code for conduct of that set of one's own people who share the same body; it is *jñātitva* and nourishes the *jñāti* relationship. These two features, shared body and a particular code for conduct, define the *jñāti* class of one's own people and distinguish it from the *kuṭumba* class.

As we stated earlier, the *jñāti* class is a definite, bounded set, although the boundaries may vary from person to person, family to family, and caste to caste. Invariably, the closest *jñāti* relationships are regarded as the shared body relationships contained in the "minimal" family: husband-wife, father/mother-son/daughter, and brother-sister. The closeness of these relationships is indicated in the fact that the term *jñāti* is most commonly used to designate one's own people outside this set of eight relationships,[6] just as in English the term "relatives" may be used in such a way as to exclude one's "immediate family." Distance among Bengali Hindus is calibrated not in terms of genealogical links, taking ego as referent, but in terms of degrees of bodily sharing taking the ancestral male as referent. For nearly every Bengali Hindu man, the par excellence *jñāti* relationship extends at least to his father's father's father (*po-bābā, prapitāmaha*) and to those sharing his body (his father's father's mother and all men descended from this couple, together with their wives). This set of *jñāti* is coterminous with the maximal family to which a man might belong. A residual *jñāti* relationship extends to those who similarly share the body of his mother's father and to the daughters descended through males from his father's father's father.

The term *sapiṇḍa* is used in the *śāstra*s explicitly to designate the largest set of par excellence *jñāti*, namely, all who share the body of the same seventh ascending ancestral male (*sapta-puruṣa*) in the father's *kula* (counting ego). While this set includes persons who would belong to the same maximal family, it also contains persons who might belong to the same *goṣṭhī*. The largest set of residual *jñāti* in the mother's father's *kula* is smaller, including only those who share the same body of the fifth ascending ancestor (including ego).

More distantly related *jñāti* in the father's *kula* are, in effect, usually classed as residual *jñāti*. The term *sakulya*, sometimes used in a general sense to mean "those of the same *kula*," is used here in a more restricted sense to designate persons sharing the body of the eighth to tenth ascending ancestor. The term *samānodaka* is used to refer to persons sharing the body of the eleventh to fourteenth ascending ancestor. Finally, persons sharing the body of more distant ancestral males are referred to as *gotraja*, "born of the same *kula*," and are normally recognized as *jñāti* only if they also share residence in the same village (*Śabdakalpadrumaḥ*, s.v. *sakulya*, *samānodaka*, and *gotraja*).

THE *KUṬUMBA* CLASS OF ONE'S OWN PEOPLE

When asked to define *kuṭumba*,[7] Bengalis state that they are persons not of their own family or clan but of other families and clans who are related by marriage (*vivāha*, *biye*). Once again, it seems that the Bengalis are using "marriage" as the defining feature of the *kuṭumba* category in the same way that Americans use it to define the class of relatives "by marriage" or "in-law." But the *kuṭumba* category is not at all the same as the American category. The structure of the *kuṭumba* category and the persons included in it make the difference clear.

The *kuṭumba* class is structured in the same way as the *jñāti* class, for it too contains a par excellence and a "residual" set. The *jñāti* and *kuṭumba* classes, unlike the categories consanguine and affine, are not mutually exclusive and opposed sets; rather, they are overlapping. The same set of kinsmen that is classed as residual *jñāti* is also classed as residual *kuṭumba*, as shown in figure 3.

Let us see how the classes of *kuṭumba* are composed. A man's wife's father, mother, brother, sister, his daughter's husband, sister's husband, father's sister's husband, his wife's sister's husband, wife's brother's wife, and so on, are included in his par excellence *kuṭumba* set (fig. 1). A married woman's sister's husband, brother's wife, and daughter's husband are classed as her par excellence

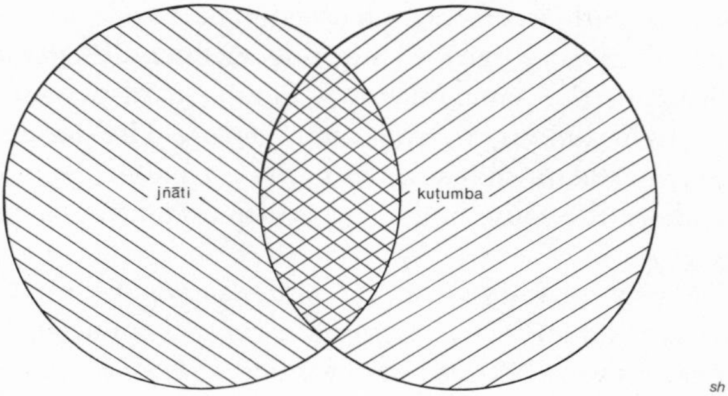

Fig. 3. Relationship between *jñāti* and *kuṭumba* classes of one's own people

kuṭumba (fig. 2). The persons who are included in the par excellence set would also be considered relatives "by marriage" or "in-law" by an American; anthropologists would call them "affines." But some persons whom an American would never class as "in-laws" are included in the residual *kuṭumba* set, namely, the very set of persons who are included in the residual *jñāti* class—for example, mother's father, mother's brother, married sisters, and married daughters. Moreover, many other persons whom an American would consider to be relatives "by marriage" or "in-law" are never included in the *kuṭumba* class. A husband and wife are not included, nor are a woman's husband's father, mother, brother, and so forth. Obviously, then, the defining feature of the *kuṭumba* class is not marriage.

The term *kuṭumba* is synonymous with the term *sambandhī*,[8] derived from *sambandha*, which means "conjoined," "tied," "bound together," and, more formally, "one who has a relationship of receiving and giving (*ādāna-pradāna*)." Many kinds of gift-giving relationships are posited in Bengali culture. What marks off the gift and acceptance relationship of *kuṭumba* and distinguishes it from all others is that it is established by the "asymmetrical" or "nonreciprocal" exchange of a human body, that is, by the gift of a daughter (*kanyā-dāna*). Thus one feature that defines the *kuṭumba* relationship is the body of the daughter (*kanyā*) who is given in marriage by her father and accepted by her husband. This daughter, whose body comes to be shared by persons of her husband's clan while continuing to be shared by persons of her father's clan, contains a particular code for conduct, *kuṭumbitā*, that sustains and nourishes the *kuṭumba* relationship and provides its other defining feature. Limits on the set of par excellence *kuṭumba* relationships, though not fixed in the *śāstra*s as they are for the *jñāti*, are informally established as, for example, in the saying, "I have no relationship (*samparka*) with the brother of father's sister's husband and the wife's brother of mother's brother" (De 1952/53, p. 658, proverb no. 6715).

Sharing and gift-giving are the features that distinguish the *jñāti* and *kuṭumba* classes from each other. Sharing or giving of a body, unlike "consanguinity" or "affinity," implies a relationship that is, translated into Schneider's American categories, simultaneously one of natural substance—the body—and of code for conduct—one enjoining sharing or gift-giving. These relationships are paradigms for the other relations a person has with his *jñāti* and *kuṭumba*.

Living Together and Sharing, Visiting and Gift-giving

The *jñātitva* code for conduct that sustains and nourishes the *jñāti* relationship is distinguished from the *kuṭumbitā* code for conduct that sustains and nourishes the *kuṭumba* relationship. The particular code for conduct that inheres in the bodies of persons classed as *jñāti* enjoins them to sustain and nourish their relationship of shared bodily substance by the *sharing* of nonbodily substances. It is considered proper for living *jñāti* of the same *parivāra* to share the same house (*bāṛi*, *gṛha*), as we have already said. Equally, the persons of a man's *parivāra*, related by the body of their common master, are supposed to share the same food, the source of nourishment for their common bodily substance. They are to share the same wealth (*dāya*, *sampatti*), the source of food. At the level of the *kula*, dead *jñāti* are thought to share in the balls ("bodies") of food (*piṇḍa*) given to them by the living *jñāti* who make up the many *parivāra*s of the *kula*. In addition, living *jñāti* of the same *goṣṭhī*, who no longer share the body of the same living master and for whom it is no longer deemed appropriate to share food and wealth, may continue to share the same house, clan deity, priest, and preceptor (*kula-devatā*, *-purohita*, *-guru*).

The actions enjoined by the sharing code for conduct are daily, regularly repeated (*nitya*) household activities (*ghar-kannā, gṛha-karma*), in which the persons of a family participate together, include eating (*khāoyā*), working (*kāj-karma*), and worshiping the gods (*pūjā*). These symbolic activities are reiterative and have as their goal the preservation of the family through the preservation of the individual bodies that share the body of the same master or *kartā*. The totality of these activities is spoken of as *saṃsāra*. Meaning "cyclic movement" or "flux," *saṃsāra* is the term that most comprehensively refers to the entire world of living beings. Its application to family activities refers to the notion that life in the family is a microcosm of life in the world at large.

Of all symbolic activities, the sharing of food (*ekānna*) most clearly and concretely expresses and sustains the shared body relationships of the persons of the same *parivāra*. Bengalis speak of the unity and solidarity of a family by saying that the persons of that family "eat from a single pot" (*eki hāṛite khāe*). A sharp contrast is drawn in Bengali culture between ordinary cooked food (*bhāt, anna*), on the one hand, and a variety of special foods (e.g., *ghī-bhāt, pakvānna, pāyas, paramānna*) on the other. Ordinary cooked food—boiled rice, lentils, vegetables—is felt to provide for full nourishment of a person's body for one day. Persons of a family who live together and eat ordinary food on a daily basis are thus thought to obtain full and proper nourishment, enabling them to carry out their daily activities. Special cooked food, which is "richer" and lasts longer, is fed to *kuṭumba*s, as we shall see.

In many anthropological accounts, and also in the census of India, a symbol closely related to food, the shared cooking hearth (*culā*), is used to define the family or household. (For a detailed discussion of definitions of Indian "families" and "households," see Shah [1974].) However, as we have shown, these symbols—the pot, the hearth, and the food emanating from them—are of secondary significance to the shared living body in defining a man's family. If persons share the body of the same living man, they have the capacity to share the same food and they should do so. The roster of such persons may include more than one married couple or not: this is immaterial to the Bengali definition of the family.[9] Sharing the same house is, for most Bengalis, of secondary importance to the sharing of food in sustaining the family. We have already discussed the fact that persons who share the body of the same master may live in separate dwellings and yet consider themselves part of his family. So long as they do so and continue to follow the sharing code for conduct that is contained in their bodies, *jñāti* sustain and nourish the "purity" (*śauca*), "respect" (*sammāna, maryādā*) and "well-being" (*lakṣmī, maṅgala*), which are the collective and common properties of their shared bodily substance. And purity, respect, and well-being are the primary concerns of the *jñāti* relationship.

One's own people who are defined as *kuṭumba*s belong to separate *kula*s, *goṣṭhī*s, and *parivāra*s; they do not live together. The *kuṭumbitā* code for conduct is the opposite of the *jñātitva* code. While it, too, inheres in the bodies of persons as *kuṭumba*s, it enjoins them to sustain and nourish their relationship of given (and accepted) bodily substance by the gift (and acceptance) of nonbodily substances. They visit one another on appropriate occasions and exchange gifts. This relationship is distinguished by special gifts, called *tattva*s (gifts that bring "news"), which move asymmetrically from the house of the bride's father to that of her husband. The preeminent examples of periodic visits between gift-giving relatives are those that occur on the occasions of Jāmāi-ṣaṣṭhī, Durgā-pūjā, and Bhrātṛ-dvitīyā. On the occasion of Jāmāi-ṣaṣṭhī the *jāmāi*, daughter's husband, is invited for a visit to his wife's father's house (*śvaśura-bāṛi*) by his wife's mother (*śāśuṛī*) and sisters (*śālī*).[10] On Durgā-pūjā the married daughter returns to the house of her father (*bāper bāṛi*).[11] On Bhrātṛ-dvitīyā brothers go to visit their married sisters in their homes (*boner bāṛi*).[12]

When gift-giving relatives visit each other, they are fed not ordinary cooked food, but special cooked food. Ordinary cooked food, the food of the family, is quickly digested and hence suitable only for providing nourishment on a daily basis. Special cooked foods, such as rice prepared with clarified butter (*ghī-bhāt, pakvānna*) or rice cooked with milk and sugar (*pāyas, paramānna*), are thought to be digested slowly and hence to nourish the body over a sustained period of time, as between visits. For this reason, the *kuṭumba*s' feeding of special food to each other expresses and sustains their exchange relationship.

Schneider's analysis of American kinship showed that the two categories of kinsmen—"blood relatives" and "in-laws"—are defined by two features. "Blood," or shared biogenetic substance, a feature drawn from the order of nature, defines the class of blood relatives; code for conduct, a feature drawn from the order of law or morality, defines the class of relatives "in-law." Our analysis of Bengali Hindu kinship shows that substance and code for conduct are also features that define and distinguish categories of kinsmen in Bengali culture. However, substance and code are not separate and contrasting things in Bengali culture; they do not belong to opposed orders of "nature" and "law" or "morality." Both categories of Bengali kinsmen are defined by the body and both are defined by code for conduct. It is not the case that the *jñāti* class is defined by "blood" or that the *kuṭumba* class is defined by "law" or code for conduct. What distinguishes them, then, is the contrast between sharing and gift-giving. The *jñāti* class is defined by shared bodily substance and a corresponding code; the *kuṭumba* class is defined by a body given and accepted in marriage and a code for conduct enjoining the giving of gifts.

It is precisely because both of these classes belong to the same order that some of one's own people may be classed either as *jñāti* or *kuṭumba*. It is a fact in Bengali culture that residual *jñāti* are related both by a shared body and by a body given and accepted in marriage. In other words, it is the presence of this feature—a body given and accepted in marriage—that marks off the residual *jñāti* and distinguishes them from the par excellence *jñāti*, those related by the shared body alone. So, for example, a mother's brother and his sister's son are *sapiṇḍa* or shared body relatives by virtue of the fact that they share bodily substance. On the other hand, they are related (asymmetrically) as givers and receivers of gifts by virtue of the fact that the mother's brother has given his sister in marriage to his sister's son's father.

The classification of residual *jñāti* is not an "either-or" issue; rather, it is a matter of stress. In those times, places, and circumstances where stress is placed on gift-giving, a relationship such as that between mother's brother and sister's son will be classed as a *kuṭumba* relationship, but where emphasis is placed on sharing, it will be classed as a *jñāti* relationship. For example, if a person goes to his mother's brother's house as a visitor, he is treated as a *kuṭumba* and receives gifts and special food. Should he become a permanent resident of his mother's brother's house, however, he is treated as a *jñāti* and shares the ordinary food and work of his mother's brother's family.

To summarize, the *jñāti* class of one's own people is defined by the sharing of a single body and by a code for conduct enjoining them to share with one another. The *kuṭumba* class is defined by the gift of a body in marriage and by a code for conduct enjoining such persons to maintain their relationship by giving nonbodily substances to one another. Both classes alike are defined through their relationship to a body. We shall return to the problem of how these classes are related to the encompassing category of "one's own people" at the conclusion of this chapter.

Love and Well-being

At one level, the sharing or giving of a body, and parallel codes for conduct enjoining the sharing or giving of other things, distinguish the *jñāti* from the *kuṭumba* class. At a higher level in this scheme of classification, relationship through a common body, whether it is shared or given and accepted in marriage, distinguishes the *jñāti-kuṭumba* class as a whole from the open-ended *ātmīya-svajana* class. Is there a code-for-conduct feature corresponding to the body, which serves as a defining feature of the *jñāti-kuṭumba* class? There is: it is a code for conduct enjoining solidarity and well-being, and it encompasses the sharing and gift-giving codes just as relationship through the body in general encompasses the sharing and giving of a body. The body, the element by which *jñāti-kuṭumba* are related, is regarded as the source of "love" (*bhālo-bāsā, prīti, prema*). Love is conceived of as an attraction, the "pulling together," or "binding" of kinsmen, which causes them to desire one another's well-being (*maṅgala, kalyāna*) and to obtain it be selflessly "caring for" (*pālana*), "nourishing" (*poṣaṇa*), and "supporting" (*bharaṇa*) one another. Following this code for conduct, kinsmen are thought to retain their solidarity with one another and thereby to obtain pleasure, delight, and gratification (*ānanda, tṛpti, santoṣa*).

For Bengalis, this love is a matter of the body and of bodily substances. The heart (*hṛdaya*), the physiological source of blood, is also thought to be the source of love, and the Bengalis use a number of expressions to indicate that they consider love to be an "essence" (*rasa*) in and of the blood and the body. A person who wants to show that he has love will say he is a "person of blood and flesh" (*rakta-māṃser mānuṣa*). When Bengalis speak of the love that kinsmen have for each other they speak of the "pull of the blood" (*rakter ṭān*) or of possessing the same heart (*eka-hṛdaya*). They will say that brothers and sisters have love for each other because they are "of the same womb" (*sahodara*) or because they are brothers or sisters of their "mother's belly" (*māyer peṭer bhāi/bon*). And they will speak of the special love that children have for their mother as the "pull of the umbilical cord" (*nāṛir ṭān*).

Fundamental to an understanding of the Bengali concept of love is the opposition between the "difficult" and the "easy." The body of every person is thought to be made up of a combination of hard and soft elements, the bones, nerves, and marrow on the one hand and the skin, flesh, and blood on the other. Similarly, semen is considered a "hard" substance, whereas uterine blood is "soft." The love of *jñāti-kuṭumba*, of which the body is the source, is believed to consist of a proper combination of difficult and easy emotional elements that more or less parallel the distinction between hard and soft physiological elements. Thus a person who speaks of "the pull of the blood," depending on the context, may be referring to the hard, difficult, and sometimes painful solidarity he has with his *jñāti-kuṭumba*, or he may be speaking of the soft, easy, and pleasant solidarity he has with them. Their code for conduct enjoins balanced participation in both difficult and easy actions. Difficult actions cause pleasure and happiness for one's *jñāti-kuṭumba* but may entail trouble and sorrow for one's self, while easy actions, which bring immediate pleasure to one's self, may entail difficulty and sorrow for some of them. Thus, the maintenance of order (*dharma*) centers concretely around the problem of sustaining the proper balance of difficult and easy relationships.

Like blood and other bodily substances, love is thought to take many different forms. The Bengali lexicon is rich in words differentiating the many subtle forms of love. The following discussion of the varieties of love necessarily involves much simplification. The kinds of love that *jñāti-kuṭumba*, the restricted set of one's own people, have for each other are defined and distinguished by birth. Birth divides all people into two exclusive and complementary genera, male and female. Union for the purpose of giving birth brings male and female together as persons of families (*parivāra*) and clans (*kula*). Birth also distinguishes people by order of birth and age. And those who give birth (*janma-dāna karā*) are distinguished from those who take birth (*janma-grahaṇa karā*). These birth distinctions are thought to give rise to two opposite kinds of love, an "egalitarian" form and a "hierarchical" form.

Egalitarian Love

Birth as a male or female gives rise to the love that *jñāti-kuṭumba* of the same sex have for each other. The foremost example of this kind of love is *bhrātṛ-prema* or "fraternal love," the love that unites brothers born of the same womb (*sahodara*). The collective activities of work and play are divided according to the distinctive capacities of men and women as persons of opposite genera, the male sex (*puruṣa-jāti*) and the female sex (*strī-jāti*). Men perform those hard or difficult (*kaṣṭa*) male actions (*puruṣa-dharma*) which have as their specific goal the structuring and perpetuation of proper order. Together, they engage in the hereditary occupation of their caste and by so doing gain the wealth and food necessary for sustaining life. Women perform those difficult female actions (*strī-dharma*) which have as their specific goal the nourishment of the body. A woman grows and nourishes a child within her womb with her body's blood. After birth she nourishes the child with the milk of her body. Because of the capacity of women to nourish, they are collectively held to be best able to prepare, cook, and distribute food. Because of their differences in attributes as two "castes" of persons, it is considered proper for men not only to work together but also to enjoy amusement together and for women to do the same. Self-gratifying play (*khelā*), unlike selfless work (*kāj-karma*), is believed to engage the soft part of a person's body.

All men of the *jñāti-kuṭumba* class, regardless of age, generation, family, or clan, are thought properly to be united by fraternal love because they are related by being born into the male genus. They share the same sex attributes and participate together in the activities appropriate to their sex. The same is true for their women. On certain occasions, which recur periodically (for example, Vijayā-daśamī, the day after Durgā-pūjā), all *jñāti-kuṭumba* of the same sex formally embrace (*āliṅgana, kolākuli*) one another, thus expressing their generic unity and equality either as males or as females. The occasions on which fraternal love may properly be expressed are, however, rare.

The marriage of a man and woman is said to make their previously unrelated bodies into the same body. Out of this union of male and female arises *dāmpatya-prema*, "conjugal love," the love that unites a man and his wife. It contains within it a code for conduct (*dāmpatya-nīti*) enjoining the man and woman to participate in the same activities as a single person. A Bengali social writer speaks in wondrous terms of the unity of husband and wife and their love:

> Marriage is a strange matter! It is the unprecedented play [*līlā*] of Fate. He unites the hearts of two unacquainted persons and

> makes them one; he joins the hands of the two together and establishes the eyes of each in the same place; and then the blood of the one mixes with the other and each passes through time sharing the sorrow and happiness of the other. The tears of the one mix with the tears of the other. Both bodies become one and in their exchange of glances the *rasa* of erotic love [*prema*] arises. Conjugal love [*dāmpatya prema*] is truly very delightful and wonderful. How this happens and why, no one can understand. It is the play of Fortune. He alone knows what honey he sprinkles on both hearts. That the *ātmā* of female and male become one through conjugal love is very beautiful and the root of purity. [Ghosh 1931, pp. 105–6]

Just as the fraternal love of kinsmen of the same sex contains a code for conduct urging both difficult and easy activities, so too does conjugal love. Sexual union for the purpose of procreating offspring, especially males, is the foremost example of the difficult work that male and female participate in together. This obligation takes priority over sexual union having as its purpose mutual bodily gratification, the prime example of the easy play (*līlā*) that male and female participate in together.

A third kind of egalitarian love is that which siblings of opposite sexes have for one another. Their sharing of the same parental body is the source of *bhrātṛ-prema* and *bhaginī-prema*, the love that unites brothers and sisters whether they are together, before their marriages, or separated by marriage. Two nineteenth-century Bengali essayists stress the equality and easiness of this relationship.

> Brother and sister receive birth in the womb of the same mother in the same house and are cared for [*lālita-pālita*] out of the same paternal love [*pitṛ-sneha*]. They both grow and improve by playing and having fun in the same lap and courtyard of their mother. The showing of mutual love [*prīti-bhāva*] among them is highly desired by everyone. [Caṭṭopādhyāya 1864, p. 14]

> The relationship of brother and sister is very sweet. From infancy they live together, gain education together, and enjoy happiness and sorrow together. For all these reasons, a deep empathy is born between brothers and sisters. Even though there is mutual competition among them, there is no envy [*irṣā*] in it. Even though they give help to one another, there is no selfishness [*ahaṃkāra*]. Even though they accept help from one another, there is no self-reproach [*ātma-glāni*]. The relationship of broth-

> ers and sisters is in origin a relationship of equality/similarity [*sāmya-sambandha*] and under all circumstances that feeling of equality [*sāmya-bhāva*] stays awake in their minds. No matter how small in age one among them may be, the feeling of equality is never completely erased. Brothers and sisters are never able to forget this fact that we are the children of the same father and mother and those who can retain specific memory of this fact are able successfully to perform their duties [*kartavya*] toward each other. [Mukhopādhyāya 1962/63 (orig., 1882), pp. 470–71]

The eloquence with which our sources speak of this form of love seems peculiar, since brothers and sisters live most of their lives separated and unable to express their love directly. The love of brother and sister stands in complementary opposition to that of husband and wife. Spouses live together on a regular, continuing basis but have few opportunities for expressing mutual, egalitarian conjugal love. After a sister's marriage, she sees her brother only intermittently when one of them is a visitor in the other's house. However, when they are together, unlike husband and wife, the mutual expression of easy and indulgent love between them is thought to be proper. Spouses must express their love for their children primarily in the difficult forms required for proper child-rearing. Brothers and sisters, by contrast, are enjoined to care for one another's children primarily in easy, pleasant, and amusing ways. However, should the sister go to live with her brother, their love is seen to become hierarchical and difficult in quality.

Hierarchical Love

Egalitarian love, the love arising from the similarities of *jñāti-kuṭumba* generated by birth, is sharply contrasted with hierarchical love, that arising from the differences among them generated by birth. All are held to be differentiated by birth into successive ordered series by generation (*puruṣa-paramparā/krama*) and into bigger (*baṛo*) and older (*jyeṣṭha*) or smaller (*choṭo*) and younger (*kaniṣṭha*) by age.

Jñāti-kuṭumba of preceding and succeeding generations are thought to be related by the gift of a body. The father and mother together are related to their children as givers of birth (*janma-dātā*), knowledge (*jñāna*), and food (*anna*). Children are related to their parents as receivers of birth (*janma-gṛhitā*), knowledge, and food. *Jñāti-kuṭumba* of the parents' generation are "modified" fathers and mothers, and all those of the children's generation are "modified" sons and daughters. The siblings of a person's father and mother are considered to be modified fathers and mothers because they share the same body with them and thus are also related as givers of birth. Similarly, the children of a person's siblings are believed to be modified children because they are related to him as receivers of birth. Even the parents of a person's spouse (together with their siblings) are regarded as modified mothers and fathers because they give a daughter to her husband or receive a daughter as a wife for their son. By virtue of the same gift (or acceptance), a person considers the spouse of his child a modified son or daughter.

Just as the *jñāti-kuṭumba* of different generations are united by a modified form of egalitarian love, so those of the same generation are united by a modified form of hierarchical love. Older siblings are nearer by birth to their parents than are younger siblings, and they are "like" parents in relation to younger siblings, who are like children in relation to them. Siblings' spouses and spouses' siblings are also united by a modified form of hierarchical love. A husband is said to give his wife a new life by making her into his "half-body." Moreover, it is believed proper for the husband to be older than his wife. Thus, even husband and wife are also united by a modified form of hierarchical love.

All of one's *jñāti-kuṭumba* who belong to senior generations or are greater in age are held to be *guru-jana*, elders, important and serious persons. Differences in generation and age among them are thought to be the source of differences in power (*kṣamatā, śakti*), knowledge (*jñāna*), wealth (*dhana*), and respect (*sammāna, maryādā*). Because of these differences between elder and younger, their love for one another takes a hierarchical form. The love that unites elders with their juniors is called *sneha*; the love that unites juniors with their elders is *bhakti*.

Among *jñāti-kuṭumba*, the foremost example of and model for the love that elders have for juniors is the love of parents for their children. Therefore, we shall refer to *sneha* as "parental love." Conversely, the love of children for their parents is the foremost example of *bhakti* and is the model for the love of juniors for their elders; we shall refer to this as "filial love." Becārām, in his glowing tribute to the Bengali Hindu father and mother, stresses the hierarchic aspect of parental and filial love. Both parents are considered to be "visible gods"; the relationship they have with their children is similar to that of god and devotee in Hinduism.

> Father and mother are themselves eminent visible deities. Their service [*sevā*] and obedience [*śuśruṣā*] is the compulsory duty and moral code of the son.
>
> Father is the agent of God in the world of the family. We gain everything—strength, virility, knowledge and morality—from our father. Depending on father's unmatched parental love [*sneha*] and unceasing kindness, we proceed down the path of life. Once we have seen father's unartificial love [*sneha-bhāva*] and desireless love [*prīti-bhāva*] we can understand our excellent father's extraordinary parental love [*vātsalya bhāva*]. . . .
>
> There is no greater duty [*kartavya-karma*] for a son than being grateful to his father. If our father had not preserved our soft body by putting food in the mouth and clothes on the body when it was helpless, we would have fallen into the mouth of death at some point. If he had not looked after the improvement of our body and mind right from infancy, if he had not kindly given us education in knowledge and morality, just where would be our matchless heavenly hopes and joys, arising from morality? Father is the single cause of all the forms of happiness and prosperity in this world; father alone is our guide on the path to the other world.
>
> Father has to endure so much trouble [*kaṣṭa*] and pain in order to support, nourish and cultivate his son and to bring about the improvement of his knowledge and morality; without him there is no way of realizing such deep feeling. [Caṭṭopādhyāya 1864, pp. 4–6]

> Of all elders, the mother is the supreme elder. Mother is to be worshipped [*pūjanīya*] and served [*sevānīya*]. She is a particular form of the qualities of God's parental love [*sneha-guṇa*]. The son has no other wisher of prosperity and good fortune on earth like his mother. The heart of his mother is his only storehouse of parental love and his mother's mind is his only shelter of selfless love [*mamatā*]. The mother is the unmatched, exemplary ground of parental love on earth. There is nothing in the world that can be compared with maternal love. The emotional essences [*rasa*] and blood of our body come from mother.
>
> Mother, a visible deity, nourishes the body of her child with milk drawn from her own body and fills the stomach of her son with half-eaten food from her own mouth. By giving her own wealth and life she causes the health of her own children and in-

> creases their strength. Mother gives a place to her child in the bed of her own womb and bears the burden of the sorrows of birth on her head.
>
> So long as the child remains in her womb, there is no end to mother's pain. Whether eating, walking, lying down, or sitting, she must endure great suffering [*kaṣṭa*]. After the child is born she worries day and night in order to preserve his body. If he becomes ill she herself fasts. [Caṭṭopādhyāya 1864, pp. 7–8]

Within the family the egalitarian love that siblings have for each other is supposed to be subordinated to hierarchical love, based upon the differences in their ages. The parental love that unites elder siblings with their juniors and the filial love that unites younger siblings with their elders is modeled after the hierarchical love that parents and children have for each other.

> The younger brother will respect the elder brother like his father. He will remain obedient to the elder always. Similarly, the elder will show the attachment of parental love [*sneha mamatā kariben*] to his younger brother and sister without distinction. [Caṭṭopādhyāya 1864, pp. 13–14]

> Big brother and big sister will dress their little brothers and sisters, feed them, wash their hands and faces, arrange their shoes and clothes, set up their toys, and play with them. When this happens, special joy [*ānanda*] is born of the father and mother and among the children fraternal love becomes properly tied.
>
> . . . All older siblings should have full responsibility for all younger siblings.
>
> If all of the children of all of the brothers of a united family are treated alike and all of the younger children are cared for by all of the older children—then the happiness and practice of morality [*dharma sādhana*] within the united family are excellent. [Mukhopādhyāya 1962/63, pp. 473–74]

The code for conduct contained in parental love enjoins elders to take care of (*lālana-pālana*), their juniors in the most general sense, by supporting (*bharaṇa*), protecting (*rakṣā*), and nourishing (*poṣaṇa*) them, thereby maintaining their well-being (*maṅgala*). The code for conduct connected with filial love enjoins juniors, in a generally similar way, to show "respect" (*sammāna karā*) to their elders in return. The head is regarded as the highest part of the body and the feet as the lowest. On certain occasions a junior kinsman displays his "inner" emotion of filial love in the "outward" form of respect to each of his elders by bowing before him (*praṇāma karā*) and taking the dust from the elder's feet (*pada-dhūli neoyā*) with his hand. The elder, in turn, expresses his interior parental love for the junior by placing his hand on the head of the junior and speaking words having as their object his well-being (*āśīrvāda deoyā*).

The "difficult" form of parental love urges an elder to care for a junior by commanding, instructing, and punishing (*śāsana karā*) him. The difficult form of filial love enjoins a younger kinsman to show his respect by obeying (*śuśruṣā*) and serving (*sevā karā*) his elders. Conversely, the "easy" form of parental love enjoins an elder to care for a junior by fondling, grooming, and placating (*ādara karā*) him. The easy form of filial love enjoins a junior to show his respect by making certain insistent demands of his elders and by begging for their indulgence (*ābdār karā*). These easy forms of hierarchical love represent a kind of "reversal" of the relationship between senior and junior.

Parents are thought to have to endure much hardship on behalf of their children and in their parental love the difficult elements are seen properly to predominate over the easy ones. Parents' parents, however, do not endure such hardship and difficulty on behalf of their children's children. The parental love that parents' parents have for their children's children allows them to engage in easy activities and to indulge them. A child's child correctly shows his respect to his parents' parents by begging them for special favors. Moreover, parents' parents and their children's children may properly show their egalitarian love to one another by playing together and amusing one another. Thus, "balanced" participation in both difficult and easy relationships is sustained, in part, by the maintenance of predominantly difficult relations between parents and children and predominantly easy relations between parents' parents and children's children. We now turn to the ways in which love—hierarchical and egalitarian, difficult and easy—is linked to the categories *jñāti* and *kuṭumba*, sharing and gift-giving relatives.

The Sharing and Gift-giving Patterns of Love

Persons who share the body of the same living male, his *parivāra* or "family," follow a family code for conduct (*gṛha-dharma*) enjoining them to live together in the same house and to share the same wealth and food by participating together in the same household work (*gṛha-karma, ghar-kannā*). Persons of the same family, his or her par excellence *jñāti*, are thought to participate in the same household work through the common living male, who is the *kartā*, the independent master of the family. He is the living seed-man (*puruṣa*), the living divinity of the family and his body is the microcosmic form of the cosmic *puruṣa* out of whose body the world was created. Just as the body of the clan's seed-man encompasses the bodies of all persons of the *kula* or clan, both living and dead, and symbolizes their unity, so the body of the *kartā* encompasses the bodies of all the living persons of his family, signifying their unity. It is the pull or attraction of the body of the *kartā* that unites the family. The sharing of his body is the source of the love that pulls their bodies toward his and his body toward theirs, causing them to desire one another's well-being. Since the *kartā* is, in relation to all other persons of the family, senior in age and generation, the fraternal and conjugal love he has for persons of his family is subordinated to his parental love.

The code for conduct contained in the parental love that the *kartā* has for all persons in his family enjoins him to care for, nourish, and support them by commanding, instructing, and punishing them. It is thought improper for the *kartā* to make distinctions among his sons or to treat his brothers' sons differently from his own sons, should they be persons of his family. Similarly, sons' wives should all be treated alike, as should their children. In relation to the *kartā*, all other persons of the family are equally his dependent juniors; all share equally in his parental love. All alike are pulled toward him by the filial love they have for him as their *kartā*. The code for conduct contained in the filial love that all persons of a family have for the *kartā* enjoins them to show respect for him by obeying and serving him. It is improper for a son and his wife to display their conjugal love before the *kartā*; when he is present, only parental and filial love should be shown. Similarly, it is not considered right for persons to engage in the easy and self-gratifying activities of chatter and amusement in the presence of their *kartā*. Instead, they must stand silent, ready to obey his orders and selflessly serve him. Thus the love that unites the family is not the egalitarian love of men for men, women for women, sibling for sibling, or spouse for spouse. While each of the forms of egalitarian love unites some kinsmen, it divides them from others. If primary stress is placed upon the love of husband and wife for one another (as it is in our own culture) it is at the expense of the larger family to which Bengalis see them as belonging. On the other hand, should primary emphasis be placed on brother-sister solidarity after either is married, it is at the expense of the conjugal relationship. The love that unites the family, as the set of par excellence sharing relatives, is the hard hierarchical love of the senior for the junior. This is the only form of love that can go on incorporating persons indefinitely without excluding any. The parental love that the *kartā* has for all of his dependents is the par excellence form of unifying hierarchical love. The difficult love that persons of the same family have for one another is also thought to be brittle. If it is not sustained through selfless participation in household work and through scrupulously fair sharing, it may turn to enmity (*śatrutā*). A Bengali proverb says, "There is no friend like a brother; there is also no enemy like a brother."

The love that unites *kuṭumba*s, as gift-giving relatives, is different in its stress from the love that unites *jñāti*s. The source of the love of *jñāti*s is thought to be in the substances—body, food, and wealth—that they share; the source of the love of *kuṭumba*s is believed to reside in the substances—body, food, and wealth—that they give or receive. The code for conduct stressed in the love of *kuṭumba*s does not require them to participate together selflessly in household work or in the difficult activities of equal sharing. Rather, it encourages them to participate together in the easy, self-gratifying activities of amusement and the easy activities of giving (or accepting) gifts. *Kuṭumba*s do not live together in the same house but visit one another's houses. The difference between the difficult love of persons in one's own house and the easy love of persons in the houses of *kuṭumba*s is made very clear in a Bengali saying:

> Hurrah! I'm going to mother's brother's house. Mother's brother's house is filled with fun, not with slaps and blows.

When a man and his wife are living in his father's house they are enjoined not to display their conjugal love before others. The wife covers her head with the end of her sari (*ghomṭā*) to display proper modesty (*lajjā*) before elders, including her husband except when they are alone together in their room. She has an easy "joking relationship" (*ṭhāṭṭā-samparka*) only with her husband's younger brothers and sisters, and then only when no elders are present. When a man and his wife visit in her father's house, however, they may properly speak together in the presence of their elders. Indeed, the hierarchical relationship of senior and junior is reversed, for the wife's father (*śvaśura*) and mother (*śāśuṛī*) receive their daughter's husband as an honored guest, a visiting deity who should be worshiped and fed. The easy form of love that a man has with his wife's sisters (*śālī*), brothers (*śālā*), and brother's wives (*śālāj*) contains a code for conduct permitting them to joke together, though even here the coarseness of the joking should be modified in accord with the sex and age of the participants. It is improper for a daughter to cover her head in modesty while she is visiting her father's house, although she must do so again when she leaves the door to return to her husband's father's house (*śvaśura-bāṛi*).

Conclusion

If it is the sharing or gift and acceptance of a human body that defines the *jñāti-kuṭumba* class of one's own people and a code for conduct enjoining their solidarity, how is the encompassing class, the *ātmīya-svajana*, defined? As we have shown, persons related by the sharing or giving of a body are also related by the sharing or giving of nonbodily substances, such as land (*bhūmi*) or words (*śabda, mantra*). Persons who have no bodily relationship may nevertheless be related by the repeated sharing or gift and acceptance of nonbodily substances on a sustained basis. Under the monistic assumption of Bengali Hindu culture, nonbodily substances as well as bodily substances may be considered as "living" and as sources and sustainers of well-being and unity. Thus the sharing or giving away of nonbodily substances may create and maintain kin relationships between persons who have no bodily connection, relationships usually treated in the anthropological literature as "fictive kinship."

For example, let us begin with the persons who live in the same house but are not related by bodily substance. We argued earlier that Bengalis distinguish between "family" and "household." All the persons of a family need not live together in the same house, and all the persons who live together in the same house need not belong to the same family. This does not mean, however, that persons not of the same family who live together are not related as one's own people. A household servant (*cākar*) and a "foster son" (*pālita-chele*) refer to the master of the house and his wife as "father" (*bābā*) and "mother" (*mā*) and are classed as their "own people." Even periodic visitors, the specialized servants of other castes such as the Barber (*nāpit*), the Washerman (*dhopā*), and the Sweeper (*methor*), belong to this class. The Brahman domestic priest (*purohita*) is also classed as "one's own person"; he is addressed not as a child, but as *ṭhākur*, "lord," by persons of the household, including its master.[13]

Persons who live together in the same neighborhood (*pāṛā*) or village (*grāma*) are related, according to their relative ages and ranks, as, for example, "neighborhood-related brother" (*pāṛā-samparke bhāi*), or "village-related father's younger brother" (*grāma-samparke kākā*), whether they are connected by bodily substance or not. Persons who are related by receiving initiation (*dīkṣā*) from the same preceptor (*guru*) are referred to as "preceptor-brothers" (*guru-bhāi*). They share with one another a powerful verbal formula (*mantra*) given to them by their preceptor and intended to protect them in their everyday lives and to guide them toward final release (*mukti*) from the world. Persons who go on pilgrimage (*tīrtha-yātrā*) together may form a more or less permanent relationship by exchanging the auspicious substances of the pilgrimage place, for example Ganges water (*gaṅgā-jala*) or flowers (*phula*) offered to a deity. Terms such as *dharma-mā*, "mother in respect of common worship," are used to designate these persons. Other persons included in this open-ended class of one's own people are "friends" (*bandhu, mitra*). The relationships of persons who are referred to by kinship terms and included in the class of one's own people, but not in any of the specific subsets mentioned so far, may be designated as "extended relationships" (*pātāno-samparka*).

One may well ask whether there is any general defining feature that would exclude anyone from the category of one's own people. Most generally, it is food (*anna*) that serves as the distinguishing mark. If food, the symbol and source of solidarity, well-being, and life, is shared or given and accepted by persons on a regular, repeated basis, it is likely that those persons will regard one another as their own people.

The class of one's own people is defined by the sharing or giving of nonbodily substances. Since the *jñāti-kuṭumba* also share nonbodily substances, they are included as a set within the larger *ātmīya-svajana* class. The usage pattern of the term *ātmīya-svajana* is the same as those of *jñāti* and *kuṭumba*. In its restricted, par excellence sense it refers to the *jñāti-kuṭumba* class, that is, to persons defined by the sharing or gift and acceptance of a body, as well as of nonbodily substances. In its unrestricted sense, *ātmīya-svajana* refers both to the *jñāti-kuṭumba* and to the unnamed "residual" category of persons related not by a body but by the sharing or giving of nonbodily substances. In its widest sense, the domain of "kinship"—that is, of "one's own people"—in Bengali culture thus includes all of a person's solidary relationships.

2 *Saṃskāra*s: The Generation and Transformation of the Body

The "Life Cycle Rites" as Symbolic Acts of Birth

So far our emphasis has been on symbols as "things," the human body, food, house, and states of being, for example, "love," and our discussion of symbolic actions has been largely confined to those "daily" or "repeated" (*nitya*) actions which have as their cultural purpose the sustenance and nourishment of solidary relationships among *jñāti-kuṭumba*. In our classification of symbolic actions we distinguish between acts of this kind and those "occasional" or "special" (*naimittika*) acts which operate either to create domains of solidary relationships or to recruit or initiate people into solidary units, statuses, or roles. In this chapter we turn to a discussion of the series of symbolic actions referred to as *saṃskāra*s, the "life cycle rites" by which solidary units and relationships among *jñāti-kuṭumba* are created.

Since the publication in 1908 of Arnold van Gennep's *The Rites of Passage*, the general class of "life cycle rites," to which the Hindu *saṃskāra*s belong, has been recognized as marking "passages" from one stage or status to another. Van Gennep (1960, p. 3) saw that most culturally defined transitions in the life of a person are marked by "ceremonies whose essential purpose is to enable the individual to pass from one defined position to another which is equally well defined." The rites of passage accomplish their objective by (1) separating the individual from his previous status (preliminal rites), by (2) putting him through a symbolic transition or passage (liminal rites), and then by (3) incorporating him into his new status (postliminal rites) (p.11). This three-step paradigm has been found to apply to ritual passages in very diverse cultures, including those of India. Many commentators have discussed rites of passage, and we do not intend to review this vast literature here. However, there are two observations that are worth repeating. Fortes asks why it is that status passages should be *ritually* marked. In illustrating his answer he says:

> The fact of birth is only a necessary, not a sufficient, condition for kinship and descent status. There is a procedure for establishing this status as a relationship with society and the ancestors; and it is focused in ritual symbolism and observance. [Fortes 1962, p. 85]

In Bengali Hindu terms we might say that a "natural" act, such as giving birth, is also at the same time a "moral" act properly accompanied by actions symbolizing both the shared body relationship and the code for conduct relationship it is thought to generate. Victor Turner (1969, p. 95) has devoted much attention to the symbols of passage of persons in the liminal phases of such rites. Among other things, he notes that such "threshold people" are usually "passive or humble" while they undergo their transition. Persons who undergo the *saṃskāra* rites will be seen to be recipients of the symbolic action. They are acted upon, and when they act themselves it is under the explicit control of some external master.

Bengali Hindus of all castes (*jāti*), clans (*kula*), and regions (*deśa*) generally state that there are ten *saṃskāra*s in a complete sequence. There is, however, no single fixed or authoritative rule governing the *saṃskāra*s for all Bengali Hindus. While both the Hindu *śāstra*s, or code books, and the Bengalis state that each caste, clan, and country may have its own rules—and, indeed they do—most Bengali Hindu families follow rules found in the *śāstra*s. Nowadays Brahman priests (*purohita*) perform the *saṃskāra*s for most Bengali Hindus. Even though the manuals (*paddhati*) these priests use provide the most "authoritative" rules for the conduct of the rituals, they themselves contain many provisions for variation. In our view, one of the most important sources of variation has been caste, with the *saṃskāra*s of higher-caste people being more elaborate and regarded as more efficacious than those of lower-caste people. Some of the major caste variations are discussed below. Finally, families of some Vaiṣṇava and Śākta communities have rules differing from the more general Vaidika rules contained in most manuals (De 1961, pp. 534–41; Woodroffe 1963, chap. 9, verses 1–284).

Variations in practice are even more widespread than variations in the rules. For example, at one extreme a family of poor economic means may perform its *saṃskāra*s in very abbreviated form, while prosperous families perform theirs on a large scale and in a very elaborate manner. Practice of a complete sequence of *saṃskāra*s does not necessarily mean that the rituals are performed on ten distinct occasions; as we shall see, two, three, and, under some circumstances, all of the *saṃskāra*s may be done on the same occasion. In some cases a family may observe a complete sequence of *saṃskāra*s only for the eldest son. In other words, the range of variation in both the rules and the practice of the *saṃskāra*s by Bengali Hindus may appear bewildering. We ourselves often despaired of discovering any general pattern when we began our investigation. However, as we compared the structures of the separate *saṃskāra*s, we became persuaded that at a "deeper" cultural level, the *saṃskāra*s done by all Bengali Hindus seem to rotate around a common core of meaning.

The word *saṃskāra* means to "complete," "prepare," "make over," "fully form," and above all, to "purify" (*śuddhi*). Every *saṃskāra* is regarded as a transformative action that "refines" and "purifies" the living body, initiating it into new statuses and relationships by giving it a new birth. A *saṃskāra* removes "defects" (*doṣa*) from the body, such as those inherited "from the seed" (*baijika*) and "from the womb" (*gārbhika*), and infuses "qualities" (*guṇa*) into it. These goals are accomplished by immersion, aspersion, or sprinkling, by touching various parts of the body, by donning new clothes, by anointing and feeding with special substances, and by the recitation of special words into the ear. Each *saṃskāra* in the sequence prepares the person for the next; all of them cumulatively prepare him for the penultimate goal of attaining "heaven" (*svarga*), "rebirth" (*punar-janma*) in a higher caste, or becoming a proper "ancestor" (*pitṛ*), in preparation for the ultimate goal of "release" (*mukti, mokṣa*) from the cycle of birth and "life in the world" (*saṃsāra*) by the separation of the person's *ātman* from his body and its union with *brahman*.

The similarity of the *saṃskāra* rites to the sacraments of Christianity is obvious. E. O. James, a renowned specialist on the sacraments, says:

> The term sacrament has become a convenient expression for a sign or symbol of a sacred thing, occasion, or event imparting spiritual benefits to participants; and such signs or symbols have been associated with eating, drinking, lustration (ceremonial purification), nuptial intercourse, or ritual techniques regarded

> as "means of grace" and pledges of a covenant relationship with the sacred order. In this way the material aspects have become the forms of the embodied spiritual reality. [James 1974, p. 115]

However, there is one important respect in which the *saṃskāra*s differ from the sacraments: The *saṃskāra*s are thought to affect the total person of the recipient and not only a "spiritual" part. Thus, for example, bathing is regarded as purifying to the "mind" (*man, manas*) and "heart" (*hṛdaya*) as well as to the exterior surfaces of the body. The head and heart are believed to control a person's body. Sprinkling the head with water and touching the region of the heart in the *saṃskāra*s are conceived of as actions that affect what Westerners would regard as both the "material" and "spiritual," or "physical" and "mental" parts of the body. The Christian sacraments are the outward and visible symbols of an inner and invisible spiritual grace. The Hindu *saṃskāra*s are outward and visible symbols of a stage of refinement or perfection (always further perfectible) that is both outer and inner, both visible and invisible.

The sequence of *saṃskāra* rites is divided into two complementary parts, the first of which leads to the procreation of a male child and the second of which makes him progressively more autonomous and capable of following his code for conduct. The first set begins with (1) *vivāha*, "marriage," which leads directly to (2) the *garbhādhāna*, or "impregnation" rite. The pregnant wife is the recipient of (3) *puṃ-savana*, "causing the birth of a male child," which may be supplemented (or replaced) by the feeding of *pañcāmṛta*, the "five immortal fluids" or symbolic semen to the pregnant wife. Later in the pregnancy, the wife receives (4) *sīmantonnayana*, "causing an easy delivery," which may be supplemented (or replaced) by the *sādh* rite in which the craving of the pregnant wife for special foods is gratified. People think that if all the rites have been done properly a son will be born, and then (5) the *jāta-karma,* or "parturition" *saṃskāra* is done. This rite is the turning point in the sequence of *saṃskāra*s; it may be augmented by the *niṣkramaṇa* or "first outing of the child." Both of these rites may be supplemented (or replaced) by Ṣaṣṭhī-pūjā, worship of the goddess Ṣaṣṭhī, who is responsible for the well-being of children, and the *aṣṭa-kalāi* ("eight beans") or *āṭ-kauṛe* ("eight cowries") ceremony in which neighborhood children are invited into the house to play and sing.

The second set of *saṃskāra*s, developing the autonomy of the son, begins with two rites that are usually done together: (6) the *nāma-karaṇa*, "naming," and the *anna-prāśana*, "first eating of rice." Following this occasion is another pair of *saṃskāra*s that is generally done at the same time: (7) *cūḍā-karaṇa*, "tonsure," and *karṇa-vedha*, "ear-piercing." Next in the sequence is the ceremony of (8) *vidyārambha*, the "beginning of study," which is followed, for boys who are not of Śūdra *varṇa*, by the (9) *upanayana*, "initiation into Vedic learning" under the instruction of a teacher (*ācārya*). This *saṃskāra* is concluded by another rite called *samāvartana*, the "return home." The final ceremony in this set is (10) *dīkṣā* or "initiation" by the *guru*. After *dīkṣā* a man is prepared for marriage and thus to begin a new sequence of *saṃskāra*s as an autonomous man in the *gṛhastha* ("householder") stage of life. (The most generally recognized Sanskrit authority for the Bengali practice of the *saṃskāra*s is the *Saṃskāratattva* of Raghunandana Bhaṭṭācārya [Chatterjee 1967]. These rules are made readily available to domestic priests in such manuals as those edited by Vidyāratna [ca. 1970] and Bhaṭṭācārya [1973/4: 421–543]. For a discussion of the *saṃskāra*s in other regions of India see Pandey [1949].)

As students of Hindu thought are aware, there are two "life-stages" (*āśrama*) a man may enter after the householder stage, those of the *vānaprastha* or "forest-dwelling" hermit and *sannyāsī* or wandering ascetic. While a few Bengali men elect to complete their lives in these ways, the great majority die as householders. There is a cycle of rites comparable to the *saṃskāras* of the living body that are to be performed by the eldest son of a man who dies as a householder. The son must first perform the *antyeṣṭi*, "final rites," centering on the *śavadāha*, "burning of the body," in which the father's gross body is burned and his subtle body is released. Then he makes a series of offerings called *śrāddha* in which the subtle body of the deceased father is nourished and rejoined with the body of his clan's seed male.

Marriage and Procreation

1. *Marriage*

First we shall examine the series of *saṃskāra*s that begins with marriage and leads to the procreation of a son. We analyze the structure and meaning of the component symbolic acts that constitute the total symbolic action of marriage (*vivāha*) in greater detail than other *saṃskāras* both because marriage is more complex than the others and because Bengalis consider marriage to be the one *saṃskāra* necessary for everyone. It is undoubtedly true that no two Bengali Hindu marriages are identical; the ceremony we examine here is a structural outline of the actions thought necessary for a complete marriage. While there are many variations among *kulas*, castes, economic levels, and regions within Bengal, all Hindu marriages seem to share this common framework. The structure of the marriage we present here is found in its entirety among "middle-income" households of the upper and middle castes, perhaps half of the Hindu population. The marriages of poorer and lower-caste families are usually contracted forms of this basic pattern. Most of the symbolic acts peculiar to particular *kulas*, castes, and regions are not discussed here.

Marriage is a symbolic action that creates a new family by uniting the separate and previously unrelated bodies of a man and woman into a single body. By unrelated it is meant that the man and woman selected to become husband and wife are not of the same *kula* (*asagotra*) and not of the same shared body (*asapiṇḍa*). This does not mean, however, that they must be unrelated in any absolute sense. In fact, quite the opposite is true. At the level of "caste" (*jāti* or *varṇa*) they must be related by shared body, otherwise the marriage will not be a proper one. The woman's body and code for conduct will not be transformed into that of her husband and they will not be able to reproduce children of the father's caste and clan. Instead, according to classical theory in the *dharma-śāstra* and elsewhere, they will generate children of a new and inferior caste. Thus marriage does not, in the Bengali view, generate a shared body relationship on the part of a man and woman who are completely unrelated. Rather, it reenacts or reestablishes at the level of the clan a shared body relationship that already exists at the caste level.

The typical ceremony consists of six segments (*aṅga*) occurring over four days: (1) *gāe halud*, "anointment of the body with turmeric," done on the eve of the auspicious day selected for the beginning of the marriage; (2) *vivāha*, "marriage," or *sampradāna*, "the complete gift," done on the first day at an auspicious time (which often turns out to occur after nightfall); (3) *bāsi-vivāha*, "leftover marriage," done on the morning of the second day; (4) *uttara-*

vivāha, "subsequent marriage," done on the second day; (5) *pāka-sparśa*, "touching of the wife's cooked rice," done on the third day; and (6) *punar-vivāha*, "consummatory marriage," which may be done on the third day or, if the bride has not celebrated her first menstruation before marriage, on an auspicious day after that first menstruation. These segments, and the segments that compose them, are seen to be a cumulative series of actions that together create a new *parivāra*. Now we turn to a description and explication of the component acts of each segment of the marriage. (Accounts of Bengali marriages are given in Bhaṭṭācārya [1973/74, pp. 421–38, 459–71, 488–95]; Chakravarti [1935]; Chattopadhyay [1964, pp. 159–77]; and Risley [1892, 1:148–52].)

The anointment of the body with turmeric. Gātra-haridra, gāe halud is preceded by the *adhivāsa*, a preliminary purification ceremony which is to be done before any of the *saṃskāra*s is performed. After bathing, the body of the groom (*vara*, "the selected one") is anointed with a preparation of turmeric in oil. A portion of the preparation with which he has been anointed should then be sent to the bride (*kanyā*, "she who desires a husband"), whose body is anointed with it after her bath. This action both seals out undesirable substances from their bodies and begins the process of transforming their two bodies into one by operating on the surfaces of their bodies. Note that at the very outset this transformation is an asymmetrical one in which the bride receives her ointment from the groom but not vice versa.

The complete gift. On the next day the second segment, *vivāha*, the marriage proper, consisting of the complete gift (*sampradāna*), is performed at the house of the bride's father. That morning, before the groom and his party proceed to the bride's house, a number of preparatory acts are done. These acts constitute the prelude on the day of any *saṃskāra*. The body of the recipient (in this case the bodies of both bride and groom) is purified by such acts as tonsure, nail paring, and bathing (*snāna, cān*). The recipient is expected to observe a fast (*upavāsa, upos*) throughout the *saṃskāra*. These acts prepare the total person for the new qualities (*guṇa*) that he will receive during the ritual. The major overall purpose of the *saṃskāra*s is to transform the recipient into a person of kingly preeminence on earth and divine preeminence in the next world. This is in part effected by dressing the recipient in new special clothing and ornaments so as to resemble deities and royalty.

In addition, the master of the groom (*vara-kartā*) and master of the bride (*kanyā-kartā*)[1] make worshipful offerings (*śrāddha*) to their respective fathers, father's fathers, father's father's fathers, mother's fathers, and mother's father's fathers. (The technical names of such *śrāddha*s are *nāndīmukha*, *ābhyudayika*, and *vṛddhi*. For a general account of *śrāddhas* see pp. 63–64.) In return for the offerings these ancestors are thought to shower down their blessings upon their living descendants.

The first day of the marriage now begins in earnest. The structure of this ritual oscillates between two poles, the *laukika*, or "popular," and the *vaidika*, or Vedic. It begins and ends with popular and often comical women's rites (*strī-ācāra*), where the theme of *kāma*, or "enjoying oneself," considered necessary in a full life, is stressed. Many of these rites take place in the women's quarters of the house, often in a bedroom. The central part of the ritual, the serious and efficacious part performed by the men, is the Vedic core of the ceremony. The rites constituting this part take place outside and stress the theme of *dharma*, the selfless code for conduct by which the world is sustained.

The groom's party (*vara-yātri*) goes in an auspicious procession (*śubha-yātrā*) to the house of the bride's father for the principal part of the first day's ritual. After the groom is welcomed (*varaṇa*) by the father of the bride, the women of the bride's side whose husbands and sons are alive (*eyo strī*), take the groom into the house and perform a number of women's rites (*strī-ācāra*). In this and subsequent phases of the ritual where the well-being (*maṅgala*) of the bride and groom is especially sought, women make the auspicious sounds *ulu! ulu!* and blow conch shells. Both these sounds are thought to be effective in purifying the impure and in driving away any malevolent beings within hearing. Thus, the women's sounds of *ulu!* and conch-shell blowing punctuate the *laukika* portions of the marriage.

After the completion of these women's rites, the central portion of the marriage, the *sampradāna*, or "complete gift," is begun. The presiding deity over this and subsequent segments of the marriage is Prajāpati, "Lord of Offspring," emphasizing the central importance placed upon procreating a child throughout this ceremony.[2]

Virtually every operation of this part of the ritual is accompanied by the recitation of *mantras*, powerful coded sounds that are believed to make the ritual action more efficacious. The literal meaning of a *mantra* need not have any particular connection with its accompanying ritual act, nor need it be understood by the participants in order to be thought effective. However, where the meaning of a *mantra* does seem of marked significance in explicating a ritual act, it will be discussed or translated.

First the bride, heavily veiled, is brought out on a low wooden seat (*piṛi*) and carried seven times around the groom. Then, at an auspicious time, the groom and bride are seated, bride at the left of the groom, facing the *kula-purohita* of the bride's father. This is done outside the house, usually in a courtyard, under a canopy. The bride and groom are then directed to view one another's faces for the first time in an act called *śubha-dṛṣṭi*, the "auspicious gaze." Their mutual gazing, accompanied by the repeated exchange of their garlands (*mālya-dāna*), is the first act by which the bride and groom, previously anointed at their separate houses, ensure their mutual compatibility in person.

The principal act of the *vivāha* segment, the *kanyā-dāna*, or gift of the bride, begins with the worshiping of the groom by the *kartā* of the bride. Acting as giver (*sampradātā*), he first offers the groom *pādya*, water with which his feet are to be washed, then an offering called *arghya*, such as is given to deities. After receiving water and rinsing his mouth with it, the groom then accepts the offering known as *madhuparka*, consisting of yogurt, sugar, milk, and honey. However, he does not eat this but, like a deity, only inhales its essence. The *sampradātā* then asks the groom to accept the gift of a bride (*kanyā-dāna*), which he does by symbolically taking her hand (*pāṇi-grahaṇa*), and the *kartā* seals the gift and acceptance by pouring water over their joined hands. He then makes other gifts, including gold and clothing, to the groom.

The uniting of the bride and groom at this stage is symbolized by the tying together of their garments (*gāṇṭ-chaṛā*) with a cloth containing fruits that stand for the children they will have together. Thus, within the marriage itself a new family is symbolically created. As we have already seen, husband and wife are considered to share the same body not because they inherit portions of the same body but because they together have the capacity to reproduce a body in common with both of theirs. The gift of the daughter in marriage is the ritual act that creates this capacity and begins their same body relationship. The tying together of the husband and wife by means of their children, which is repeatedly enacted in the marriage, symbolizes the body of their child in whose birth their same body relationship will be realized. At the same time, the gift of the daughter also initiates the *kuṭumba* relationship between a man and his daughter's husband at the level of bodily substance. The honoring of the groom by the bride's father, and the selfless gifts of wealth, clothing, and so forth, that he gives the groom, symbolizes the almost total asymmetry of their gift-giving relationship as *kuṭumba*s. These actions, carried out for the first time here, realize the code for conduct that they are to observe from this day on.

The serious work of the first day is now completed and the remainder of the night is given over to lighthearted activities. The couple, still tied together, are conducted to a bedroom called the *bāsar-ghar*. Women from the bride's side gather there and again perform women's rites (*strī-ācāra*). They play games and joke with the bride and groom, trying to keep them awake all night. As a price for taking away one of their number, the groom is teased relentlessly by the women. Even if the bride and groom have reached puberty, they are not to have sexual intercourse on this night, since their marriage is not yet completed.

Leftover marriage. Early on the morning of the second day the bride and groom are taken out to the site of the previous day's rites. A condensed version of the marriage is reenacted. This is known as *bāsi-vivāha* or *bās-biye*, "leftover marriage" and summarizes the preceding segment before the next step is undertaken. It is an intermezzo which divides the first part of the binary structure of the marriage from the complementary second part.

The subsequent marriage. The principal ceremony of the second day is the *uttara-vivāha* or "subsequent marriage." The preceding segment of the marriage was performed by the *purohita* of the bride's father using substances and implements of his house; the *uttara-vivāha* is performed by the *purohita* of the groom's father and uses articles from his house.[3] Although the overall structure of the *uttara-vivāha* is the same as that of the *vivāha*, the *uttara-vivāha* is more complicated. Like the *vivāha*, it begins with (1) a *śubha-yātrā* or "auspicious procession," and (2) a *varaṇa* or "welcome." The central part of the second day's rites, parallel to the gift of the bride on the preceding day, is (3) the *kuśaṇḍikā*, a form of Vedic worship, which is made up of six segments: (*a*) the *agni-sthāpana*, or "establishing the fire" of the bride and groom, (*b*) the *aśmākramaṇa*, or "treading on the stone," (*c*) the *sapta-padi gamana*, or "taking of the seven steps" together by husband and wife, (*d*) the *gotra-parivartana*, or "changing of the *gotra*" of the wife to that of her husband, (*e*) the *bhojana*, "feasting," or *hṛdaya-sparśa*, "touching of the heart," and (*f*) the *sindūra-dāna*, or "giving of vermilion" by the husband into the parting of his wife's hair. The *uttara-vivāha* concludes with (4) the *kāla-rātri*, the "black" or "mortal night." The objective of this segment is twofold: it initiates the husband and wife into the householder stage of life in the house of the husband's father and transforms the wife into a woman of her husband's *kula*. It also "interiorizes" the "same body" relationship of the husband and wife.

The groom's party takes the bride in an auspicious procession (*śubha-yātrā*) to the groom's house where she is welcomed (*varaṇa*) by the women of the groom's side whose husbands and sons are alive. The central segment of the *uttara-vivāha* is the *kuśaṇḍikā*, a particular type of vedic worship in which oblations of clarified butter (*ghī*, *ghṛta*, *ājya*) are offered into a fire. These are done by the husband and wife together or on their behalf by the *purohita*. These offerings unite the couple with the power of the gods. Their new codes for conduct as husband and wife, previously latent, become realized. Thus the rituals acted out by the husband and wife together are efficacious symbols: not only do they symbolize their new status, but by acting out that status, the bride and groom realize their new roles.

The fire of the husband and wife is established (*agni-sthāpana*) for the first time. This fire is different from the ordinary cooking fire of the house and is established outdoors. They are seated before it, wife on her husband's left, facing the *purohita*. With his right hand the husband offers a series of oblations into the fire while his wife touches his right shoulder. (The main offering here is the *ājya-homa* or oblation of clarified butter.) Before marriage a man and woman are thought to be incomplete persons, not yet fully capable of following the code for conduct (*dharma*) of householders. As we have seen, the sharing of food cooked over the same fire is the foremost symbol of the ongoing unity of the persons of a family. Among Hindus no food may be eaten until it has first been offered to the deities. Thus, before the daily meal is taken, a householder (*gṛhastha*) and his wife as female householder (*gṛhiṇī*), acting as a single person, offer some of their ordinary food to the deities. The first oblations made into the *kuśaṇḍikā* fire initiate the newly married man and wife into their roles as male and female householder, causing them to enter the householder stage of life (*āśrama*). This initiatory offering of food made by the newly married couple is not done in the ordinary manner using the ordinary substances of daily life; it is done with the extraordinary fire established outside the house and with special foods. The oblations are repeated many times and are accompanied by powerful Vedic *mantra*s. These extraordinary measures are taken to insure that the sought-for transformation not only takes place but is made permanent. As we stated earlier, the wife is considered to be the half-body (*ardhāṅginī*) of her husband. The asymmetry of her status as sharer of her husband's body is symbolized by her participation in these oblations as "co-worshiper" (*sahadharmiṇī*) with her husband.

Next come two interrelated actions, the *aśmākramaṇa*, or "stepping on the grinding stone," and the *lāja-homa*, "the offering of parched rice." In the *aśmākramaṇa* the husband and wife stand together, and he makes her step on a grinding stone with her right foot. Subsequently the offering known as *lāja-homa* is made. Some parched rice (*lāja, khai*) from the groom's house is placed in the bride's hands, her husband pours *ghī* on this, and she offers it into the fire. After repeating both these actions a number of times, the husband and wife together circumambulate the fire (*agni-parikramaṇa*).

When they are alone, husband and wife may demonstrate their egalitarian, conjugal love for one another. When they are among others, however, they should display only hierarchical love. The wife is to have "filial love," *bhakti*, for her "master" and he is to have "parental love," *sneha*, for her. Moreover, the filial love for her husband is supposed to be her primary *bhakti* relationship, stronger than the *bhakti* she has for her own parents and elder siblings. Stepping on the stone is a symbolic act that strengthens the *bhakti* of the wife—as the accompanying *mantra*, asking that the wife be as "firm (*sthira*) as a stone," suggests. The offering of parched grain that follows is the first time the woman acts out her role as a married worshiper in her husband's house, one major purpose of which—again indicated by an accompanying *mantra*—is to bring long life to her husband and her new *jñāti*.

The central portion of the *kuśaṇḍikā* is the *sapta-padi gamana* or "walking of seven steps." Standing behind his wife, who pushes the grinding stone before her, and holding her right hand, the husband makes her take steps through each of seven circles (*maṇḍala*); he walks behind pushing her right foot with his. As they proceed the husband recites *mantra*s such as these:

> One step for increase [*iṣ*], become devoted [*anuvratā*] to me; let us two obtain many sons and let them attain old age. Two steps for vigor [*ūrjja*], become devoted to me. . . . Three steps for the increase of wealth [*rāyas-poṣa*]. . . . Four steps for comfort [*māyobhava*]. . . . Five steps for children [*prajā*]. . . . Six steps for seasonal regularity [*ṛtu*]. . . . Seven steps for companionship [*sakhā*]. [Bhaṭṭācārya 1973/74, p. 494]

After completing the seventh step, the husband recites this *mantra* to all who have viewed the marriage: "This wife (*vadhū*) is a bringer of well-being (*sumaṅgalī*); come together and view her. Bestow good fortune (*saubhāgya*) on her and return home." The groom next recites this *mantra*, "Let the All-gods (Viśvedeva) unite our two hearts with water." As he does so a relative approaches the couple and pours (*abhiṣeka*) water from a pot onto their heads. Then, still standing, the husband grasps his wife's hand and recites additional *mantra*s concerning their new life together in his father's house.

> I take your hand for good fortune, that you may live with me as husband/master [*pati*] to an old age. The gods Bhaga, Aryaman and Savitṛ have given you to me in order that we obtain mastery of a household.
>
> Become an empress [*samrājñī*] in relation to your husband's father [*śvaśura*], become an empress in relation to your husband's mother [*śvaśrū*], become an empress in relation to your husband's sister [*nanandā*], become an empress in relation to your husband's brother [*devara*].
>
> Let your heart [*hṛdaya*] be placed in my sphere of conduct [*vrata*], let your thoughts [*citta*] be in accord with my thoughts, take kindly to my words; let Prajāpati join you to me. [Bhaṭṭācārya 1973/74, p. 434]

The husband concludes the *sapta-padi* segment with six oblations of *ghī* into the fire, each time placing a drop of the remainder on his wife's head. As he does this he states that with a full oblation he extinguishes everything productive of defects (*pāpaka*) with respect to every part and function of her body (*sarvāṅga*)—her hair, eyebrows, eyelashes, teeth, and forehead, her sight, her crying, her character, her speech, her laughter, her hands, her legs, her genitals, and so on.

The seven steps which the husband makes his wife take with him in this ceremony symbolize the wished-for prosperous and fulfilling journey that the couple will take through life together and have the effect of making the wife his half-body for life. The stone the wife pushes again symbolizes the lifelong devotion she will have for her husband. Many Bengalis consider this to be the part of the marriage ceremony that makes their relationship as man and wife permanent and irreversible. The sprinkling of clarified butter on the bride's head acts to seal this transformation in her bodily substance. The sprinkling by a relative effects the union of the bride and groom by symbolically giving them birth together as a single person. Marriage is also regarded as the second birth of a woman. In removing the elements that produce defects from his wife's body, a man is preparing that body to be born again with a new set of qualities (*guṇa*) appropriate to a person of his *kula*.

The next segment is the *gotra-parivartana*, or "changing of the wife's *gotra*." After gazing at the polestar (*dhruva*), the husband makes his wife recite the following *mantra*: "You are eternally fixed (*dhruva*); may I become eternally fixed in the *kula* of my husband." They then gaze at the star Arundhatī, the devoted wife of the star Vasiṣṭha, after which the husband recites this *mantra*: "As the sky is eternally fixed, the earth is eternally fixed, the entire world is eternally fixed, and these mountains are eternally fixed, so this woman is eternally fixed in her husband's *kula*" (Bhaṭṭācārya 1973/74, p. 435). Immediately after this, the wife pronounces the husband's *gotra* and salutes (*namaskāra*) him by pressing the palms of her hands together and bowing her head. He returns the salute with a blessing of long life for his wife. Then a married woman whose husband and son are alive sprinkles (*abhiṣeka*) them with water from a pot with a mango sprig, once more symbolizing their birth together as a single person. Again, this segment ends with a *homa* offering.

The next segment is called the *bhojana*, "feasting," or *hṛdaya-sparśa*, "touching of the heart." Having recited this *mantra*, "With the superior bond of food (*anna-pāśa*), the subtle thread of life (*prāṇa*), with this knot I securely tie your mind (*manas*) and heart (*hṛdaya*) to mine," the husband eats some boiled rice (*anna*) and feeds the remainder to his wife. He then requests Prajāpati, the presiding deity of the marriage ceremony, to bring about the unity (*aikya*) of his and his wife's hearts. Toward this end, he recites the following *mantra* to his wife: "Let your heart be my heart, and let my heart be yours" (Bhaṭṭācārya 1973/74, p. 435). Ordinary food, boiled rice, is the symbol of living together. The heart is the symbol of love, *prīti*, in all its forms. Here food is used to effect a bodily change in the husband and wife, "interiorizing" their same body relationship by causing their hearts to be exchanged.

Next, married women whose husbands and sons are alive seat a boy who has not yet been tonsured on the wife's lap and place fruit in his hand. The husband then makes a series of oblations known as the *dhṛti-homa* which he concludes by offering a twig dipped in *ghī* into the fire. Pronouncing the name of her husband's *gotra*, the wife bows to her husband's elders. This segment is again concluded by the groom's making oblations into the fire. As during the ceremony of the previous day the garments of the bride and groom were tied together with a cloth containing fruit, so too the seating of a boy on the lap of the bride symbolizes her giving birth to a child. However, on this occasion the emphasis is not upon the child whose body unites the bodies of husband and wife but rather upon the son as *vaṃśa-dhara*, "holder of the bodily substance of the *kula*." Procreating a son is not only the symbolic action that completes the same body relationship of husband and wife and begins their minimal family, but also the action that perpetuates the *kula*.

The next segment is the *sindūra-dāna*, or "the giving of vermilion." After a series of oblations called *caturthī-homa*, the couple stands to the north of the fire and the husband sprinkles his wife's head with a purifying mixture of *ghī* and water. He then makes a mark with vermilion powder (*sindūra*) in the parting of her hair and pulls the end of her sari down over her face. This concludes the *kuśaṇḍikā*, the serious, daytime, Vedic portion of the *uttara-vivāha*. In this action the husband symbolically enters his wife's womb and activates her uterine blood for the purpose of producing a son for his family.[4] By placing this mark on her forehead for the first time and pulling down her veil, the husband causes her to be his chaste and loyal sexual partner for the rest of their common life. She will continue to wear a vermilion mark, emblematic of her status as a reproductive woman. If her husband dies before her she must remove this vermilion mark and avoid any red bodily adornment, symbolically deactivating her reproductive capacity.

On the night of the second day, as on the first night, the husband and wife are not to have sexual intercourse. But on this night, known as *kāla-rātri*, the "black" or "deadly night," the husband and wife are not even to see one another: the husband is to spend the night with the men and the wife with the women of the family.[5] The separation of the husband and wife on this night is an efficacious symbol of the subordination of their egalitarian, conjugal love for one another to the parental and filial love that unites the family. The *uttara-vivāha* is not complete until this night is over.

Touching of the wife's cooked rice. The next major segment of the marriage, known as *pāka-sparśa* or *bou-bhāt*, "touching of the wife's cooked rice," takes place on the third day. After the new wife has bathed, the husband's mother conducts her into the kitchen. There she is introduced to the articles used in cooking and made to act out her role as woman in her husband's house by cooking the rice for a meal. The food she has cooked is distributed to the persons of her husband's family and to his *jñāti*. Once they have touched and eaten this food, this segment comes to an end.

In preceding parts of the ceremony, emphasis was placed upon the "special" (*naimittika*) actions uniting a wife with her husband and his *kula*. In the *pāka-sparśa* segment the emphasis is shifted to regularly repeated (*nitya*) unifying actions. The sharing of ordinary cooked food, of which boiled rice (*bhāt, anna*) is the symbol and foremost example, is the par excellence regularly repeated action symbolizing the unity of the family. The foremost duty of a wife is to prepare food for her husband and the other persons of the family. In this ceremony, for the first time she enacts her role as a wife in her husband's house by cooking the rice for the daily meal. By accepting the rice she has cooked, her husband and his *jñāti* acknowledge that she is now a *jñāti*, a wife of the *kula*. This segment of the marriage has the purpose of beginning to bring the wife into a "normal" relationship in the household, out of her extraordinary status as a bride.

The consummatory marriage. The night of the third day is called the *śubha-rātri* or "auspicious night." A bed adorned with flowers (*phula-śayyā*) is prepared for the couple, who are beautifully dressed and garlanded. Women of the husband's family conduct the couple into this room. Husband and wife take prepared betel leaves and exchange them with one another seven times, finally placing them in one another's mouth. This ends with an exchange of garlands. Meanwhile, the women have been continuously making jokes relating to sexual intercourse and conjugal love. *Punarvivāha* or *punarbbiyā*, the "consummatory marriage," may or may not take place after the *śubha-rātri* activities have been completed. If the new wife has not had her first menstrual period (*ṛtu*, metaphorically referred to as *rajodarśana*, "the appearance of pollen"), she may return to her father's house until it occurs. If, as is common nowadays, the bride has already menstruated, they may proceed immediately to the consummatory marriage which may, in this case, include the next *saṃskāra* in the cycle, *garbhādhāna*, or "impregnation." Figure 4 illustrates schematically the main segments in the structure of the marriage and their oscillation between Vedic and popular parts.

2. *First Impregnation*

The *garbhādhāna*, or "first impregnation" *saṃskāra*, is the symbolic action undertaken by the husband and wife with the object of begetting a male offspring. On the early evening of an even-numbered day[6] from the fourth to the sixteenth day after the appearance of the wife's menses,[7] the couple sits with the wife to her husband's left. The husband introduces himself and his wife to the gods, using their *gotra* name, and states that they desire a son. He then worships the goddess Ṣaṣṭhī, who is responsible for the well-being of children. After the preliminary rites (*adhivāsa*), the husband and wife together make an offering, accompanied by a *mantra*, to the sun (*sūryārghya-dāna*), a great source of generative power. The wife shares (again asymmetrically) in her husband's activation by the sun by touching his hands as he holds the offering.

Next, the husband touches the region of his wife's navel (or genitals, or heart, or head, in different versions of the ceremony) and recites a *mantra* requesting that a good son endowed with long life, a holder of his *vaṃśa*, be born, and that his wife's pregnancy be characterized by every form of well-being and be without obstacle. Then a woman whose husband and son are alive, or a male child, gives the wife a mixture of *pañcagavya* ("the five products of the cow": milk, yogurt, clarified butter, dung, and urine) to drink for the purification of her body (Bhaṭṭācārya 1973/74, pp. 438–39; 471; 495–97; 519–21). In some castes and regions, the image of a boy is made from rice paste. This is placed inside her clothing near her navel and is dropped down and out from her sari, thus explicitly enacting the conception and birth of a male child, which is the goal of this ceremony (Bose, ca. 1929, pp. 7–8).

For the Bengalis, the procreating of a child is premised upon certain definitions of the nature of the human body and its functioning. The human being as a male (*puruṣa*) is distinguished from the female by the capacity to produce semen (*śukra*), often referred to metaphorically as "seed" (*bīja*). The distinctive feature of a human being as a female (*strīpuruṣa*) is her capacity to produce uterine blood (*ārtava*) in her womb (*garbha*), often referred to metaphorically as the "field" (*kṣetra*). Both semen and uterine blood are the products of a series of physiological transformations. Food (*anna*) is the external source of a person's body. When it is eaten it is transformed progressively into digested food (*rasa*) and then into blood (*rakta*). Blood, the internal source of a body's nourishment, is the source of both semen and uterine blood. Within a person's body, blood turns into flesh (*māṃsa*), flesh into fat (*meda*), and fat into marrow (*majjā*). The marrow in a male person turns into semen; in a female it turns into uterine blood. Thus the semen in a male and the uterine blood in a female are both highly concentrated forms of blood. And these are the human substances from which a person's body is generated. (This theory, widely attested to in Ayurvedic medical sources, is also generally held in Bengal. See, e.g., Chakraberty [1923, pp. 49–53].)

The generation of a body is thought to be the result of a particular birth or generative act, "generation in a womb" (*garbhotpādana*), an act that takes place between a man as genitor (*janaka*) and a woman as genetrix (*jananī*) when they unite or combine (*saṅga, yoga*). Particles from the body of the genitor—semen (*śukra*)—are thought to mix with the particles in the body of the genetrix—uterine blood (*ārtava*)—to form an embryo (*garbha*) in the stomach (*peṭ*) of the genetrix. The semen, which comes from the phallus (*liṅga*) of the genitor, is regarded as the source of the "hard," structuring parts of the body: bones, nerves, and marrow. The uterine blood, which comes from the womb (*yoni*), is regarded as the source of the "soft," unstructured parts of the body: skin, flesh, and

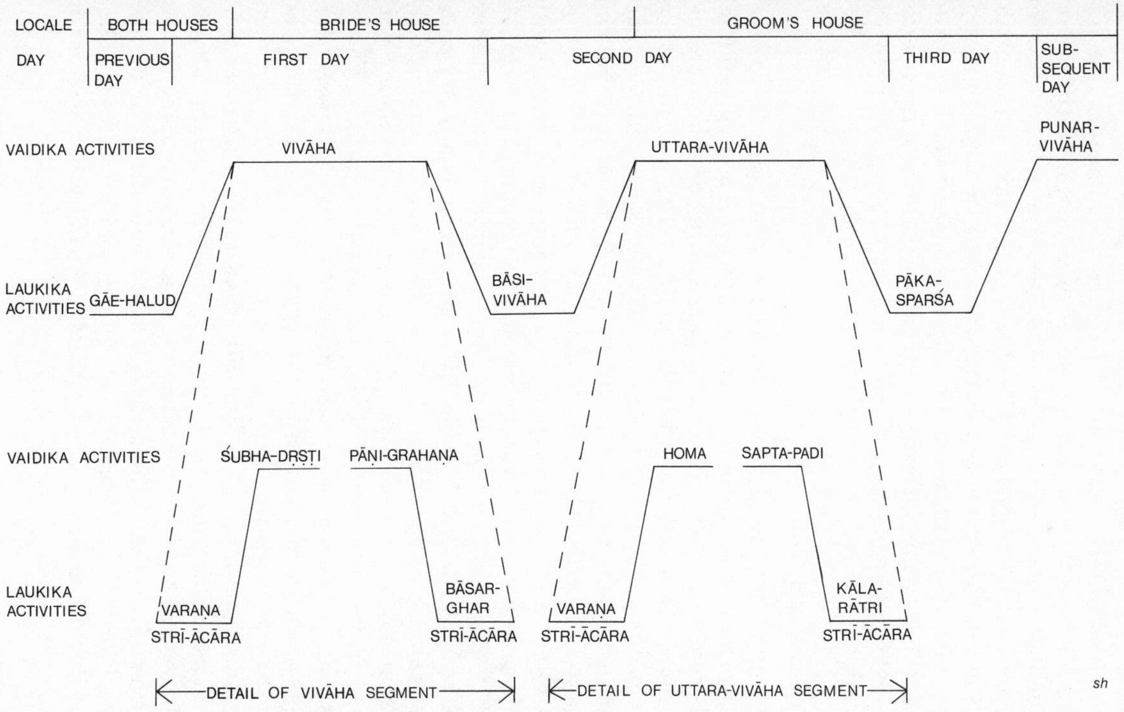

Fig. 4. Schematic outline of the structure of Bengali Hindu marriage

blood. The sex of the offspring is thought to be determined not by the presence or absence of male or female substances but by the proportions of these substances. If semen predominates, the offspring will be male, that is, a producer of semen; if uterine blood predominates, the offspring will be female, that is, a producer of uterine blood. (An equal mixture of semen and blood is thought to result in the conception of a hermaphrodite.) Conception is supposed to take place on an even-numbered day because it is believed that semen is stronger than uterine blood on these days; the reverse is thought to be true on odd-numbered days (Sengupta 1913/14, pp. 23ff.).

3. *Procreating a Son*

The object of the next *saṃskāra* in the sequence, the *puṃ-savana*, is to cause the birth of a male child by strengthening the semen (*śukra*) or seed (*bīja*) that is mixed with the wife's uterine blood (*ārtava*) or planted in her field (*kṣetra*). The husband effects this, according to one text, by causing his wife to drink some yogurt (symbolic semen) to which "seeds"—two *māṣa* beans (a lentil) and one grain of barley—have been added (Bhaṭṭācārya 1973/74, p. 497). Other texts instruct the husband to squirt water mixed with various potent substances up his wife's nose (Bhaṭṭācārya 1973/74, pp. 471–72). This *saṃskāra* is no longer performed as a separate ritual by most Bengali Hindus. Even in the eighteenth and nineteenth centuries it appears to have been performed separately only by Brahmans. More widespread has been a brief ceremony performed in the fifth month of the wife's first pregnancy. This is known as the giving of *pañcāmṛta*, five "immortal" (*amṛta*) liquids—yogurt, milk, clarified butter, sugar, and honey. After the pregnant wife is fed this symbolic semen, she eats some rice pudding (*pāyas*) out of the same dish with a boy and five married women who have sons (Bose, ca. 1929, p. 9). The effectiveness of feeding the wife seminal foods rests on the assumption that when foods are ingested they are ultimately converted into semen or uterine blood. If the wife eats seminal food at this stage it increases the likelihood that the seminal portion of her child will be increased and it will thus be a male.

4. *Easy Delivery*

Next follow a pair of ceremonies designed to bring about the easy delivery of the child. The first of these, a Vedic ceremony called the *sīmantonnayana*, "the parting of hair," is to be performed in the sixth or eighth month of pregnancy. Just as the husband had earlier, in the marriage ceremony, symbolically effected sexual intercourse with his wife by placing a vermilion mark in the part of her hair, so now he effects a smooth delivery by parting her hair with auspicious and fertile items such as unripe figs and *darbha* grass (Bhaṭṭācārya 1973/74, pp. 440–42; see also Leach 1958). The second, popular ceremony, called *sādh*, "the gratification of cravings," is performed in the seventh or ninth month and, unlike the Vedic prenatal ceremonies, may be repeated on the occasion of each pregnancy. Here the bodily needs of the pregnant woman are met by her husband's mother and other female *jñāti* with gifts of clothing and choice foods (Bose, ca. 1929, p. 10).

The symbolism of this first group of *saṃskāra*s emphasizes the union and fertility of the husband and wife. The preparation of the wife for an easy delivery begins a transition from attention to the well-being of husband and wife to attention to the well-being of their child, who concretely embodies and symbolizes their one body relationship.

Parturition, Maturation, Death, and Rebirth

Birth (*janma*) is the pivotal action in the cycle of *saṃskāra*s; it is by birth that a person is said to receive his body. Since the body is the central symbol and defining feature of "kinship" in Bengali culture, birth is the central symbolic action and therefore highly valued. At the same time, Bengalis are aware of the fact that birth is a dangerous, painful, and "messy" process. This physiological aspect of birth is suppressed in Bengali culture. Yet, as the action through which a person receives his body, birth is the paradigm for all of the other *saṃskāra*s. The rites that follow the parturition *saṃskāra* all purify and refine the body, helping it mature and become more autonomous by symbolically giving it rebirth.

5. *Parturition*

A number of preparations and rites, some Vedic, others popular, surround the birth of a son, making it, along with the marriage and final rites, the most elaborate of the *saṃskāra*s. The Vedic ceremony known as the *jāta-karma*, "acts of worship" (*karma*), done at the time of "parturition" (*jāta*), contains two major segments. After a son is born, but before the midwife (*dāi-mā*) cuts the umbilical cord (*nāṛi*) and his mother feeds him milk, the child's father offers food to his ancestral fathers. Having entered the room where the child has been born (*sūtikā-gṛha*) and viewed his face for the first time (*mukha-darśana*), he cleanses (*mārjanā*) the baby's tongue first with powdered rice and then with a piece of gold with honey and clarified butter on it. At the same time he also chants *mantra*s into the ears of his son. This part of the ceremony, the *medhājanana*, not only effects the removal of inauspicious defects the child might have inherited from his parents, but also causes the quality (*guṇa*) of intelligence (*medhā*) to be born (*janana*) in him. The second segment, the *āyuṣya-karma*, "the act causing long life," brings another quality, long life, to the son as his father again recites *mantra*s into his ears. Having in this way strengthened the child by infusing him with divinely charged substances and efficacious sounds, the father then orders the midwife to cut the umbilical cord and the mother to feed him her more ordinary breast milk (Bhaṭṭācārya 1973/74, pp. 473–75). The period of birth impurity begins when the umbilical cord is severed (see Appendix 3).

A child is thought to be separated from his mother at this moment; yet even though he becomes a separate entity he is still said to have the same body as both of his parents, for his body contains particles of his father's and his mother's bodies. The child obtains his heredity from his parents and shares it with them. Hence, a boy is believed to resemble his father in appearance and a girl her mother. Thus the same body relationship in Bengali culture, as represented by the parent-child relationship, is formulated in concrete terms. Another Vedic ceremony, *niṣkramaṇa*, "the first outing of the child," though meant to be performed in the third or fourth month, is usually combined with the *jāta-karma*. Of minor importance, its purpose is to unite the child for the first time with the world outside the house in a manner conducive to his well-being (*maṅgala*) by showing him Candra, the moon god (Bhaṭṭācārya 1973/74, pp. 503–6). The performance of the *jāta-karma* (together with the *niṣkramaṇa*) as a separate ritual accompanied by its own *homa* oblations, the feasting of Brahmans, relatives, and the poor, seems again to be confined largely to Brahmans. More widely distributed is a ceremony performed on the sixth lunar day (*ṣaṣṭhī*) after birth, Ṣaṣṭhī-pūjā (more colloquially, Ṣeṭerā-pūjo), "the worship of Ṣaṣṭhī," the goddess in charge of the well-being of children. Her worship is intended to have the same effect as the *jāta-karma* in bringing well-being and long life to the child, and families of the higher castes have often engaged the family priest to perform it as well as some of the Vedic trimmings such as *homa* oblations. Some believe that the god Brahmā comes the night after Ṣaṣṭhī-pūjā and invisibly but indelibly inscribes the child's entire future on his forehead. In order to ensure that the future be as good as possible, some families make the child touch his forehead to a strip of cloth embued with the divinely charged foot dust of Brahmans (Bose, ca. 1929, pp. 14–15).

On the eighth day after the birth of a son another ceremony, strictly popular, is often performed. It is called *aṣṭa-kalāi* or *āṭ-kauṛe*, "eight beans" or "eight cowries." Neighborhood children are invited in, and as they dance, sing, and play, eight kinds of sweets and other foods, toys, and prizes are distributed among them. The association of the newborn son with these delighted children is supposed to effect a pleasant childhood for him (Bose, ca. 1929, p. 15; Rāya 1903/4, pp. 65–66, 106–7).

6. *Naming and Feeding*

The next *saṃskāra*, the *nāma-karaṇa* (or *nāma-rākhā*), "naming," is to be performed on the tenth night after birth or, more commonly, on the occasion of the *anna-prāśana*, discussed below (Bhaṭṭācārya 1973/74, pp. 444–45). The father holds his child and recites two names into his ear. One of these, a regular name, has historically been the name of a Hindu deity considered appropriate for the child in accord with his day of birth, zodiacal sign, and so on. The second name, a *ḍāka-nāma*, or "calling name," is the name by which his senior relatives will address him (Rāya 1903/4, pp. 107–8). (A son may also be given a *gupta-nāma*, "secret name," to protect him from envious or jealous beings [Bhaṭṭācārya 1973/74, p. 502].) This ceremony further marks the child off from his parents while at the same time uniting him with a deity who will take special interest in his future welfare.

The *anna-prāśana* (or *mukhe-bhāt*), the first feeding of solid food, is to be carried out in the sixth or eighth month for a boy and in the fifth or seventh month for a girl (Bhaṭṭācārya 1973/74, pp. 445–46). As in conception, even-numbered months are considered more conducive to maleness, odd-numbered to femaleness. This ceremony has a number of purposes. Coming as it does around the time the child begins teething, the first feeding of solid food begins the weaning process. Up to this time the child has been fed its mother's milk. From now on it will increasingly take solid food. More important, the child's relationship with the gods and with his *jñāti* is inaugurated on this occasion in the following way. The mother's brother (or a *jñāti* of his father's *kula*) places the child in his lap and feeds him a bit of boiled rice (*anna*) which has been mixed with the powerfully charged leaves (*prasāda*) of a chosen deity. Then the child is placed in a palanquin and carried to the places of the deities in the neighborhood and made to bow his head (*praṇāma*) before them. After returning home, the child is placed in its mother's lap and the invited *jñāti*, especially those supposed to have a gift-giving relationship with the child, make gifts (*yautūka*) to it and extend their blessings (*āśīrvāda*) (Bose, ca. 1929, p. 18). Boys and girls are also introduced to their adult sex roles at this time. For example, the Kāyasthas—writers and accountants by caste occupation—place items such as inkpot, pen, and paper before a boy and a container for vermilion, emblematic of her future role as a married woman, before a girl (Rāya 1903/4, p. 76).

7. *Tonsure and Ear-piercing*

Next come two more *saṃskāra*s that are, like the *nāma-karaṇa* and *anna-prāśana*, often combined. These are the *cūḍā-karaṇa* or "tonsure" and the *karṇa-vedha* or "ear-piercing," to be performed in the third year of a boy's life or in a subsequent odd-numbered year up to the fifteenth (Bhaṭṭācārya 1973/74, pp. 446–48). As a result, they may be performed either before or after the *vidyārambha*, "the beginning of study," scheduled for the fifth year (Bhaṭṭācārya 1973/74, pp. 455–56). In any case, both were to be performed before the boy's *upanayana*, his initiation into Vedic learning (if a Brahman) or before marriage (if a Śūdra). Although both of these are designed to effect a long life and well-being for the child, they can take on a different significance depending on the year in which they are performed and their place in the overall sequence of *saṃskāra*s. Performed in the third or fifth year, the *cūḍā-karaṇa* effects the completion of the child as a person. Before the child's third year he has not been fully weaned. He is not expected to control his bodily eliminations or to eat in an appropriate manner with the other persons in his father's house (Rāya 1903/4, p. 77). Should the child die during this period, his relatives do not incur the same period of impurity they would after his second birthday. The tonsure ceremony marks the completion of the early "socialization" process by purifying and strengthening his head, considered the most important and vulnerable part of his body. Our account of the *karṇa-vedha* as a ceremony performed after the fifth year is given below.

8. *Beginning of Study*

The *vidyārambha*, also known as the *hāte-khaḍī*, "chalk in the hand" ceremony, is to be performed in the fifth year, before a boy begins the learning of the Bengali script and other livelihood skills such as arithmetic. The *purohita* of the family worships Sarasvatī, the goddess of learning (*vidyā*) and performs a *homa* oblation. Then he, or another Brahman who knows how to write well, draws the characters of the alphabet on the ground and causes the boy to trace over them with a piece of chalk (*khaḍī*), thereby transferring writing skills to the boy (Bose, ca. 1929, p. 19; Rāya 1903/4, p. 108). Historically, this was an important ceremony for upper-caste boys who were not initiated into Vedic learning. In the early nineteenth century boys continued their schooling for about ten years—that is, up until about the age of puberty (Adam 1941 [1835, 1838], pp. 230, 240).

9. *Initiation into Vedic Learning*

Among some of the higher Śūdra castes, the *karṇa-vedha*, or ear-piercing, of a son appears to have become a kind of parallel to the Brahman *upanayana* and, like that rite, gives a rebirth to the recipient, marked by the pouring (*abhiṣeka*) of water on his head at the end of the ceremony. Performed in the ninth, eleventh, thirteenth, or fifteenth year—that is, before the age of sixteen when a boy is thought to attain puberty (*vayaḥsandhi*, literally the "juncture" in one's lifetime)—it generally came at the end of a boy's period of study. The belief was that the piercing of the boy's ears made him competent to make minimal offerings of water to the deities.

The next and most famous of the *saṃskāra*s is the *upanayana*, the act by which a youth is "led" (*nīta*) to a teacher (*ācārya*, *guru*). It is to be performed between the ages of seven and fifteen. Once he has passed into his sixteenth year, the year of puberty, his competence to undergo the *upanayana* is lost. Its purpose is to initiate a Brahman man into *dvija* or "twice-born" status.[8] The code for conduct of a twice-born Hindu enjoined him to recite the Veda and perform Vedic acts of worship using the powerful Vedic *mantra*s.

This is effected by making the boy undergo a "second birth," during the course of which he is invested with a sacrificial thread (*upavīta*; more colloquially, *paitā*). Once the requisite preliminaries—anointing the boy's body, shaving his head, performing *śrāddha*, offering *homa* oblations, and so on—have been completed, the father gives his son over to the teacher. Having accepted him, the teacher inducts him into the "life-stage" (*āśrama*) of a *brahma-cārī*, "he who practices (*cārī*) the Veda (*brahma*)." This is effected by touching his navel, stomach, heart, and shoulders while chanting the appropriate *mantra*s. The teacher then invests him with the sacrificial thread which he is to wear as a *brahma-cārī*, or student. The code for conduct of a *brahma-cārī* enjoins him to learn the Veda from his *ācārya* and, all the while staying in his house, to live austerely by seeking alms (*bhikṣā*).

In the next part of the ritual the teacher makes the boy act out this code for conduct. First, he causes him to learn the *mantra* pertaining to Savitrī, presiding deity of the sun. He will recite this *mantra*, also known as the *gāyatrī*, every day of his life as he bathes facing the rising sun. Next, the teacher hands him a staff, emblem of a mendicant's life, and instructs him to beg first from his mother and father and then from other men (Bhaṭṭācārya 1973/74, pp. 448–52). The length of time spent as a *brahma-cārī* may extend from a portion of one day to several days or, in those rare cases where a Brahman boy actually undertook to learn a Veda and its appendages, several years.[9] In any case, the end of this period is marked by the performance of another *saṃskāra*, the *samāvartana* or "return home." This rite was also referred to as the *snāna* or "bath," the name of its central feature, the act by which this change is effected. After making an offering (*añjali*) of warm water mixed with sandalwood paste (*candana*) and the seven items making up *sarvauṣadhi* ("every type of herb"),[10] he pours some of it (*abhiṣeka*) on his own head. He then discards the girdle, staff, and thread which marked his life as a *brahma-cārī* and dons new silk garments and a new sacrificial thread, ornaments, garland, and shoes. This change of clothing symbolizes and completes his second birth. He now has the same status as his teacher, which the latter recognizes by worshiping (*pūjā*) him with the *arghya* and *pādya* offerings (Bhaṭṭācārya 1973/74, pp. 453–55, 485–88). The boy has left the first life-stage, that of the *brahma-cārī*, but he has not yet entered the life-stage of a householder. This he will not do until his marriage. In the meantime he takes on the "liminal" status of a *snātaka* Brahman, "one who has bathed." He has the knowledge with which to worship the Vedic gods using a fire and *mantra*s; yet without a wife he is not a complete person and hence not fully competent to make the actual offerings. Since Brahmans in Bengal have usually performed the *upanayana* of their sons just before their marriages, the period of life spent as a *snātaka* was of minor significance.

10. Initiation for Release

Another "initiation rite," the *dīkṣā*, or "instruction," is usually undergone by Hindus between the ages of seven and fifteen, or in any case before marriage. This rite falls outside the sequence of bodily *saṃskāra*s. The primary stress in these *saṃskāra*s is on the attainment of the three goals of worldly life—worship (*dharma*), wealth (*artha*), and enjoyment (*kāma*)—by creating families and uniting persons with the gods of the Hindu pantheon. The primary stress in the *dīkṣā* is on attaining the goal of *mukti*, release of the person's particular self (*jīvātmā*) from worldly life itself and its union with the universal self (*paramātmā*). For this purpose it is believed necessary for everyone to become the filial devotee (*bhakta*) of a particular "chosen deity" (*iṣṭa-devatā*); in order to do this he must become the "disciple" (*śiṣya*) of a *guru* who will provide him with a special "seed" (*bīja*) *mantra* and instruct him in the code for conduct by which he may ultimately attain release. The *dīkṣā* is the necessary sacramental rite that accomplishes all this:

> If one does not accept initiation, the particular self (*jīvātmā*) does not wear her lucky thread (*maṅgala-granthi*). Just as the undertaking of the life of the householder, of life in the world is not completed if one does not marry, if two particular selves (*jīvātmā*) are not auspiciously joined together, so, in the same way, if instruction in a *mantra* does not take place, there is no way for the *jīvātmā* and the universal self (*paramātmā*) to unite. [Bhaṭṭācārya 1973/74, p. 526]

The *dīkṣā* proceeds as follows: After the preliminary worship of the gods (*adhivāsa*) and the offering of oblations into a fire (*homa*) have been completed, the initiate declares his intent: "I, So-and-so of Such-and-such *gotra*, desirous of obtaining the results of worship [*dharma*], wealth [*artha*], enjoyment [*kāma*], and release from these three [*mokṣa*], shall accept my own *mantra* in the form of this syllable through the deity So-and-so" (Bhaṭṭācārya 1973/74, p. 544). Then the *guru* draws a design (*yantra*) in an appropriate vessel, invokes the chosen deity and worships it, recites the *mantra* he will give, and offers *homa* oblations to the deity 108 times.

Next the *guru* seats his disciple across from him, chants the *mantra* about to be given him into a jar of water 108 times and pours the water (*abhiṣeka*) onto the head of the disciple. This symbolically effects the birth of the initiate as a filial devotee of his chosen deity and as a disciple of the *guru*. The *guru* then ties up the tuft of hair on top of the new disciple's head and chants the *mantra* over it 108 times. A kind of reenactment of the tonsure ceremony, this protects and completes the initiate as a devotee and disciple. The *guru* then infuses the disciple with the divine power he needs in order to attain release by chanting the seed *mantra* into his ear three times. Having received his *mantra*, the disciple prostrates himself before the *guru*, who is considered a living incarnation of his chosen deity, and praises him as such. The *guru* then pulls him up by the hand and blesses him, saying, "Arise, child, you are released [*mukta*], become endowed with the proper rituals. May fame [*kīrti*], fortune [*śrī*] and handsomeness, long life, strength, and health always be yours, O son" (Bhaṭṭācārya 1973/74, p. 545).

The cycle of *saṃskāra*s of the living body from birth through initiation prepares the body of a man to enter the householder stage of life (*gṛhasthāśrama*), which he does at the time of his marriage. Marriage is the last of the *saṃskāra*s of the living body and also the first. It is interesting that death and the accompanying rites, although considered to be a *saṃskāra*, are not included in this cycle. The reason for this seems to be the great stress that Bengali Hindu culture places on the continuity of life and the perpetuation of the clan. This emphasis is carried to its logical extreme in the death rites, which, as we shall see, are symbolically treated as a form of life-giving rebirth.

Death and Rebirth

The *saṃskāra*s of the living body, as a whole, are opposed to a kind of *saṃskāra* of the dead body, the *antyeṣṭi* or *śavadāha*, the "final rites" or "burning of a body." It transforms bodily substances and their codes for conduct, and it generates relationships between the living and the dead. These transformations can be understood only if one appreciates the Hindu conception of the human body's constitution. A living body consists of two complementary parts, a gross (*sthūla*) body (*śarīra*) and a subtle (*sūkṣma*) body. During the process in which the gross body is formed, its complementary subtle body is thought to combine with it. The subtle body consists of mind (*manas*), the five sense organs of knowledge (*jñānendriya*): eyes, ears, nose, tongue, and skin, and the five organs of action (*karmendriya*): voice, hands, feet, anus, and genitals. The subtle body, which is contained in the gross body, in turn contains an even more subtle substance, the conscious self (*ātman*).

At the time of death, the gross body of the deceased is burned. Normally the eldest son of a man is responsible for burning his body and for making a series of offerings to him during the following year. The responsible man leads a procession to the cremation ground, where he causes the body to be placed on the funeral bier and covered with firewood. After a prayer for the well-being of the deceased, he lights the pyre, first placing a burning stick in the dead man's mouth. The subtle body of a person, as modified by his actions (*karma*) in life, is thus released from the gross body. The period of death impurity begins once the body is burned (see Appendix 3). A portion of this subtle body is attracted to a new embryonic gross body to which it is suited, and it is reborn. Another portion, that which concerns us here, persists in subtle form and is known as the *preta-śarīra*, or "departed body."

The *preta* body must be nourished as a living body; this is done on a number of occasions during the year after death. During the period of death impurity, the responsible man must offer the *preta* of the deceased ten balls of cooked rice (*pūraka-piṇḍa*). When the death impurity has been removed, the first of a series of rites called *ekoddiṣṭa śrāddha*s is performed. The term *śrāddha* is derived from *śraddhā*, "faith," and indicates an offering made with faith toward the dead; *ekoddiṣṭa* means "intended for one," indicating that the offering is made to the deceased alone, rather than to the many ancestors who are fed and worshiped at other *śrāddha*s. (Such *śrāddha*s are performed, for example, before the *saṃskāra*s; see the discussion of marriage above, p. 42. For a more detailed discussion of funeral rites and *śrāddha*s see M. Bhattacharyya [1972].) The central symbolic action of the *śrāddha* is the "gift of a body of food" (*piṇḍa-dāna*), in which the responsible man offers a ball of cooked rice, symbolizing the body of the deceased and feeding that body at the same time.

The initial (*ādya*) *śrāddha* is done on the day after death impurity has been removed. It is followed in each subsequent month, on the lunar day of the death, by a monthly (*māsika*) *śrāddha*, and in the sixth and twelfth months, by special "six-monthly" (*ṣānmāsika*) *śrāddhas*. On each of these occasions the *preta-śarīra* is fed with *piṇḍa*s intended exclusively for its benefit. Finally, on the first anniversary of the death, the *piṇḍa* for the *preta* is mixed with the *piṇḍa* offered to the ancestors (*pitṛ*) in the *sapiṇḍīkaraṇa śrāddha*. After this offering is made, the deceased is thought to take his place among the ancestors and to rejoin with the body of his clan's seed male. In return for the gifts of *piṇḍa*s that a dead man receives, his sons are to receive his "property" (*dāya*, *viṣaya-sampatti*).

As the *śrāddha* of a dead person separates him from the living, it also separates the living from each other. When a man dies, the single *parivāra*, or family, that was united by his body is thought to be transformed into the separate families of his sons, his living descendants. The separation of families is regarded as proper; it preserves and perpetuates the clan by regenerating its living parts in each generation. Recall that the body and love of the living *kartā* are the features that both define and unite a "joint family." When the *kartā* dies, the family that he united ceases to exist so far as Bengalis are concerned. This does not mean that a joint family is instantaneously divided on the death of its *kartā*, but rather that the process of division begins then. Indeed, the presence in the family of the deceased *kartā*'s widow may be the cause for continued joint living for a period of several years. As the "half-body" of the *kartā*, she provides her husband's family with a kind of "liminal" existence while she is alive. If her sons are young, she may even play the role of master temporarily. However, it is expected that the oldest son will become *kartā* until the division of the family is completed. As the family of the father is transformed into the separate families of his sons, so too the wealth that they receive from him is divided (*dāya-bhāga*) among the sons in equal shares. Henceforth his sons and their family dependents will have separate houses and separate wealth, and they will cook and eat separately.

Bhūdeva Mukhopādhyāya, in his essay on the Bengali family, succinctly states both the necessity and the difficulty of the proper separation of a family after the death of its *kartā*:

> After the marriage of the brothers and the death of the father and mother, a fraternal split may begin. But if the paternal wealth

> is clearly divided in a well-cared for family, this almost never happens. If there is a genuine unity of minds among brothers, their wives will not become rivalrous toward each other. The roots of quarreling among brothers' wives are first, the quarrels of sons and second, the quarrels of daughters. These are two very common matters and with very little care they can be prevented. . . . If there is a possibility of ill-feeling, the only means of prevention is to become separate in food [*pṛthaganna*]. Doing this by mutual agreement of the brothers is best; it is improper to give rise to ill-feeling, and the one who has the least means or the most children should properly be the one to propose the separation of food. But even after they have become separate in food the unity of mind of the brothers can always be fully maintained, but if it is not, then faults arise in their natures. Even after they are separate in food, mutual assistance will continue, their empathy will remain undivided, there will be joint consultation in particular matters, and the performance of rituals [*anuṣṭhāna*] in common will continue. Brotherly love [*saubhrātra*] and sisterly love [*saubhāginya*], these are everlasting relationships. Purity is effected by preserving this relationship and no cause for selfishness arises. By not preserving it, the destruction of purity occurs and popular criticism arises. [Mukhopādhyāya 1962, 3:474–75]

Birth (*janma*) is an act by which a person obtains his body and his code for conduct. In our own culture the term "birth" is generally used to denote the "natural" act of parturition. In Bengali culture, however, "birth" (*janma*) is defined quite differently. Bengalis postulate no absolute separation between natural and moral orders or material and spiritual orders and thus do not separate a natural from a spiritual or supernatural birth, such as is symbolized by the sacrament of baptism in Christianity. Similarly, there is no sharp contrast drawn in Bengali culture between such things as a "natural" birth and a "spiritual" or "moral" rebirth.

Two of the *saṃskāra*s we have discussed are explicitly said by Bengali Hindus to involve a "second birth" (*dvijāti*) or "rebirth" (*punar-janma*). This will come as no surprise since there is much discussion of the "twice-born," and of "rebirth," "transmigration of souls," "metempsychosis," and "reincarnation" in Western literature on India. Much of this discussion rests on the dichotomy drawn in Western cultures between a material "body" and a spiritual "soul." As we have seen, Bengalis do make a contrast between a "gross body" (*sthūla-śarīra*) and a "subtle body" (*sūkṣma-śarīra*), between "conscious self" (*ātman*) and "body" (*śarīra*), and between "mind" (*manas*) and "body," but they do not conceive of them as belonging to different parts of existence. The opposition between the gross and the subtle body succinctly states the nonduality of these entities, for "gross" and "subtle" do not distinguish "matter" and "spirit," but are "more" and "less" terms that modify a single entity, the body. Just as there is no contrast between a material body and a spiritual soul, so too in Bengali culture there is no contrast between natural acts of birth and moral or spiritual acts of birth.

Any act that changes the status of a person by transforming his body (and his inherent code for conduct) may be classified by Bengalis as an act of birth. All the *saṃskāra*s meet this qualification. If all of the *saṃskāra*s do the same thing, one might ask why they are not all classified as marriages or initiations, for example. Birth in the restricted sense of parturition is central for the simple reason that it is the act by which a person becomes established on earth (*bhūmiṣṭha haoyā*). The other *saṃskāra*s merely change his earthly status. Even the *saṃskāra* of the dead body is considered to be a form of birth or, more accurately, a rebirth.

3 Bengali Kinship Terminology

The Language of Kinship in Bengal

The earlier chapters of this account were focused on an analysis of the classes of kinsmen who are related to a person by sharing the same body or by the gift of a body in marriage or by the sharing and giving of nonbodily substances coded for love. But the terms *ātmīya, svajana, jñāti, kuṭumba*, and so on, are not the only terms used in Bengali to designate kinsmen. There are many terms used to denote classes of kinsmen who have some *particular* kin relationship. These are terms such as *bābā*, "father," *jeṭhā*, "father's elder brother," and *śvaśura*, "spouse's father." Anthropologists have generally made two assumptions about such terms: First, they think it possible to isolate these terms in the language of the group or society under study and to describe them as constituting the "kinship terminology" of that language.[1] Second, they have assumed that the "pattern" of such a group of terms in some way reflects a unitary structure of social relations or of underlying cultural categories.[2] Consequently it has been considered almost obligatory that a study of kinship include an attempt to analyze the structure of the terminology itself.

The first difficulty encountered in such attempts is the problem of defining what the kinship terminology or lexicon is in a given group or society. For example, the terms to which we have devoted most of our attention here—*ātmīya, svajana, jñāti, kuṭumba*, and so on—are not usually included in any of the attempts to analyze the structure of the North Indian terminologies (e.g., Dumont 1962; Vatuk 1969; Leaf 1971). The failure to state what terms like these mean has led to much confusion. On the other hand, some terms that do not have strict "kinship" meanings are unquestioningly included in lists of kinship terminology. For example, there is no term in Bengali that means "male spouse" and nothing else. The term *svāmī* means "husband," but it also means "lord" or "master." It is true that the husband in Bengali culture is the lord or master of his wife; yet there are masters who are not husbands, for example, Swami Vivekananda. Many other examples of equal ambiguity can be found in Bengali.[3] Clearly, then, it is difficult if not impossible to draw a tight boundary around a set of terms called a kinship terminology.

The other major difficulty centers on the question of just what "structure" or "patterns" the classification of the kinship terms is supposed to reflect or represent. G. S. Ghurye (1955, pp. 8, 215–39), for example, is confident that the structure of the terminology reflects the opposition between consanguines and affines. Madan (1965, p. 229–37) has argued in his study of Kashmiri kinship (following Radcliffe-Brown) that the classification of the kinship terms, although occasionally problematic, is "by and large, consistent with the attitude and behaviour of kin to each other." Dumont (1966, pp. 90–103, following Lévi-Strauss and a study of the Dravidian terminology in South India) tried to see whether the classification of kinship terms in Uttar Pradesh could be seen as a reflection of the classing of people as wife-givers and wife-takers for the purpose of perpetuating marriage alliances. Vatuk (1969) has subsequently shown that this mode of classification leads to even more complications than Dumont originally suspected. Leaf (1971, pp. 551–52) notes the obvious distinction between "patrilateral" and "matrilateral" sets of terms. In her study of Sanskrit kinship terms, Karve (1965, p. 69) tried to show that the classification of kinship terms parallels the distinction between "one's own people" (*svajana*), who are relatives by birth, and "bound kin" (*sambandhin*), who are relatives by marriage.

The only significant work on kinship terms in Hindu Bengal, that of Jyotirmoyee Sarma (1951), which contains a valuable discussion of usage patterns, largely avoids the issue of the patterning of the terminology. Mukherjee's (1962, pp. 48–50) account of the somewhat peculiar kinship terminology of the Rajbanshis of North Bengal attempts a componential analysis of terms but assumes that the terms distinguish "consanguines" and "affines" as defined in Western cultures.

With the possible exception of Karve, analyses of North Indian kinship terminology have rested, in some way, on the assumption that the basic pattern reflects the opposition between "consanguines" and "affines." For a long time we too labored unde misapprehension that the terms patterned out in this way. We already shown that the two categories of kin, *jñāti* and *kuṭumba* not correspond to the categories "consanguines" and "affines." The whole question of the patterning of the terminology must therefore be reformulated. Does the Bengali kinship terminology pattern out into the classes of *jñāti* and *kuṭumba*? Is the transformation by marriage of *jñāti* (sharing) relationships into *kuṭumba* (gift-giving) relationships "reflected" in the terminology? Finally, does the overlapping of the *jñāti* and *kuṭumba* categories appear in the patterning of the terminology?

It is extremely difficult to isolate a clearly bounded set of terms that have purely "kinship" meanings. As we shall see, the set of terms that passes for a "kinship terminology" is in fact a conglomerate, containing words which all have multiple meanings. That is, the terms used to denote kinsmen are mostly at the intersections of several different systems of classification, such as sex, age, and generation, as well as the sharing and giving of food, knowledge, land, and so on. These criteria combine with the "kinship" criteria, birth and the sharing or giving of bodily substance, to constitute the "kinship terms."

Since the "kinship terms" are a conglomerate semantic domain, the "patterning" of these terms may be expected to reflect not one uniform structure but a number of overlapping and intertwined structures. Close to two hundred words, many of them synonyms, can be selected out of the Bengali lexicon and characterized as "kinship terms." One distinction that accounts for many of these synonyms has to do with the special relationship between the Bengali language and Sanskrit. Lexemes in Bengali are sorted into two categories depending upon their relationship with Sanskrit lexemes. Those identical to words in Sanskrit are classed as *tatsama* ("equivalent to that"); words originating from Sanskrit but not identical are classed as *tadbhava* ("derived from that"). From an "objective" philological point of view, some Bengali words fall into a third class made up of words not derived from Sanskrit. There is a tendency among Bengali authorities to class many terms from this latter category as *tadbhava*.

There is a further distinction between words considered appropriate to the various spoken styles of the language and those used in the written styles. We regard all of these forms, *tatsama* and *tad-*

bhava, spoken and written, as "legitimate" uses of the language. Virtually every kinship term in Sanskrit is also used as a kinship term in Bengali, and we attempt to take account of this in our analysis. If there are many levels of usage in Bengali, there are also many regional and dialectal variations in its pronunciation. Since these variations are of little consequence with respect to the kinship categories of Bengali Hindu culture, we ignore them here. In short, we concentrate upon those terms most universal in their distribution, the Sanskrit ones, and those of "standard colloquial" Bengali, the style now taught in schools throughout the region. Finally, it is the meaning and usage of kinship terms that is of primary importance to us. We engage in philological analysis to illuminate semantics, not as an end in itself. That is, linguistic patterning that is unrelated to the pattern of kinship meanings is not treated as either significant or troublesome.

The Patterns in the Kinship Terminology

Basic Terms

First we consider the terms used to designate the eight classes of kinsmen Bengalis consider most closely related by birth: *bābā* ("father"), *mā* ("mother"), *bhāi* ("brother"), *bon* ("sister"), *chele* ("son"), *meye* ("daughter"), *svāmī* ("husband"), and *strī* ("wife").[4] These eight terms, denoting the persons of a minimal family, form a whole set that is differentiated into four pairs by the symbol of birth. The mother and father (*mā-bābā*) are related to their son and daughter (*chele-meye*) as "givers of birth" (*janma-dātā* and *janma-dātrī*). Their son and daughter are "receivers of birth" (*janma-gṛhita*) in relation to them. The husband and wife (*svāmī-strī*) are together givers of birth; brother and sister (*bhāi-bon*)[5] are together receivers of birth. Birth is the action that generates relationships of bodily substance among persons. Various synonyms of these terms convey the notion of bodily relationship. For example, the father is spoken of as "genitor" (*janaka*) and the mother as "genitrix" (*jananī*); their children are said to be born of their body (*deha-ja*) or of their self (*ātma-ja*). Brothers and sisters are characterized as born "of the same womb" (*sahodara, sagarbha*). Finally, the husband and wife are spoken of as "having the same body" (*eka-deha*), for they together generate the body of their child.

According to the "pure" kinship criteria, the set of eight terms is differentiated not into eight but into four classes; that is, they are not distinguished by sex. It is only when the criterion of sex or gender is combined with the pure kinship criteria that each of the four pairs is differentiated into male and female. These sex criteria are "built into" the words themselves. Other criteria beyond kinship and sex are "built into" some of these eight terms as well as some of their many synonyms and modifiers.

As we have shown, birth as a kinship criterion relates persons by bodily substance. However, birth also relates people in other ways: as male and female, as persons of senior and junior generations, and as older and younger. Sex, generation, and age are criteria in relationships among persons who are not kinsmen as well as among those who are; thus, these are not pure kinship criteria. However, sex, generation, and age intersect in the formation of the terms for kinsmen in Bengali. The combination of these three criteria is reflected in the eight basic terms and their use. For example, the terms *chele* and *meye* are used not only to denote persons related as "son" and "daughter" but also for "boy" and "girl," as males and females born in a junior generation but having no "kinship" connection. The term *strī* is used to denote not only a person related as "wife" but also a "female." Thus, it should be clear that "kinship terms" refer not only to kinship roles but to roles defined by sex, generation, and age as well. In addition, the sharing and giving of other than bodily substances also generates named relationships. For example, one's father is said to be his *anna-dātā* (food-giver), *jñāna-dātā* (knowledge-giver), and *bhaya-trātā* (deliverer from fear). One's genitor is not the only person, however, who can perform these roles. Other elder males related by birth and bodily substance, such as one's father's father, father's brother, elder brother, or wife's father, may also fulfill them. In addition, some persons not related as *jñāti* or *kuṭumba* may also perform these roles. For example, kings and gods are characterized as "food-givers" and "deliverers from fear" and one's preceptor (*guru*) is his "knowledge-giver." These are persons who are classed as *ātmīya-svajana* although not as *jñāti-kuṭumba*.

Keeping in mind the conglomerate character of the roles defined by kinship terms, let us analyze the meaning and use of the eight terms. The term *bābā* is used by a man's child both to address him and to refer to him. This term implies the respect emanating from the filial love (*bhakti*) that a child has for his father. The term *mā* is used in the same way as *bābā* and with the same implication of respect. Other terms used as synonyms for the word *bābā* include, in addition to *janaka* (genitor), the *tatsama* forms *pitā* or *pitṛ* and *tāta*, as well as the *tadbhava* form *bāp*. Besides *jananī* (genetrix), the term *mā* has the *tatsama* form *mātā*. Another pair of terms, *ṭhākur* and its feminine form *ṭhākruṇ*, meaning "embodied deity," are also used in restricted contexts as synonyms of *bābā* and *mā*.

A parent may refer to his children as "my son" (*āmār chele*) and "my daughter" (*āmār meye*) but addresses each of them by a special "address name" (*ḍāka nāma*) given within the family.[6] A parent may also address his son as *bābā* and his daughter as *mā*. Both the use of the address name and the terms *bābā* and *mā* by a parent indicate parental love (*sneha*) in its easy form (*ādara*). In addition, the reciprocal use of the terms *bābā* and *mā* between parents and children is a statement of their unity and identity as persons of the same parental body.

The term *āmār* ("my") *svāmī* is used by a woman to refer to her husband and *āmār* ("my") *strī* by a man to refer to his wife. A husband and wife may address one another by the untranslatable term *ogo*, which implies their mutual conjugal love. Since conjugal love is to be subordinated to the unifying hierarchical form of love, husband and wife may not use the term *ogo* in the presence of elders but should both use parental terms. Thus, a man should address his wife as, for example, *Gobinder mā* ("mother of Govinda"), and she should address him as *Gobinder bābā*. Privately, a man may address his wife by her name, since she is younger than he. A wife may never use her husband's name, however, even to refer to him, implying great respect appropriate to her filial love for him.[7]

A person may refer to any male born of his own father and mother as *āmār bhāi* ("my brother") and to any female of that kind as *āmār bon* ("my sister").[8] The most common usage pattern for both reference and address avoids the terms *bhāi* and *bon*. Instead, terms denoting senior and junior siblings according to the order of their birth are used. *Dādā* ("elder brother") and *didi* ("elder sister") are used by younger siblings both to refer to and to address elder siblings. The reciprocals of *dādā* and *didi* are the address names of younger siblings. In addition, an elder sibling may address a younger brother as *dādā-bhāi* and a younger sister as *mā*. A younger sibling may address or refer to an elder brother by his address name plus the term *dādā*, or more commonly its shortened form, *dā*, as for example, *Kālu-dā* ("elder brother named Kālu"). An elder sister may similarly be addressed and referred to by her address name plus *didi* or *di*.

Differences of age or relative "bigness" and "smallness" among kinsmen are also indicated in terms of reference by the use of such "nonkinship" adjectives as *baṛo-* ("big") and *choṭo-* ("small"). Where more than one distinction of age needs to be made within a set of siblings of the same sex, other adjectives may be used, such as *mejo-* ("middle-born") and *sejo-* ("third-born"). Thus, for example, a man might describe his eldest brother as *baṛo bhāi*, his second elder brother as *mejo bhāi*, himself as *sejo bhāi*, and his youngest brother as *choṭo bhāi*.[9] However, he will address any and all of his elder brothers as *dādā* and distinguish among them by compounding, for example, *baṛ-dā*, *mej-dā*. Younger brothers are addressed by name.

Consistent with the stress placed on parental and filial love, the address terms are used to subordinate brotherly love among siblings to the hierarchical form of love. We did not include the term *dādā* (and its feminine form *didi*) in the list of basic terms because *dādā* is a *tadbhava* form of the word *tāta* ("father"). Thus, just as a parent communicates his parental love by addressing his child by his address name, so an elder sibling indicates his parental love in the very same way. Conversely, a younger sibling communicates filial love to an elder sibling by addressing him as *dādā* or *didi*. Finally, the use of *dādā* for a younger brother and of *mā* for a younger sister once again displays the identity of persons sharing the same parental body.

Modifiers are used to distinguish "abnormal" relationships in the minimal family from those which are "normal." Many "abnormal" relationships may be generated when a man takes a second wife. He uses the modified form *dvitīya-pakṣer* ("of the second marriage") to distinguish the second wife and her children from the *prathama-pakṣer* ("of the first marriage") wife and her children. The wives of such a man refer to one another as *satīn* or *sapatnī* ("co-wife"). A woman distinguishes the children of her husband's other wife (whether that wife is living or not) from her own children by the use of the prefix *sat-* ("step-") before the terms for son and daughter. These children may refer to her as *sat-mā* or *vimātā* ("stepmother"). The term *sahodara* ("of the same womb") is used to distinguish siblings born of the same mother from those who are not. Siblings born of the same father but of different mothers are referred to as *sat-bhāi/-bon* or *vaimātreya bhāi/bon* ("half-brother/sister"). A man distinguishes an adopted son from a "son born of his body" (*aurasa-putra*) by the use of a modifier such as *dattaka-* or *poṣya-* ("adopted"). A daughter's husband who comes to reside with a sonless man in his family is designated as *ghar-jāmāi* ("daughter's husband of the house"), a term which is perhaps best understood as "marital son."

Terms for Jñāti

Virtually all recent attempts to discover patterns in North Indian kinship terminology have been premised upon the assumption that the major cultural categories in the terminology are "consanguines" or "agnates" and "affines" or "in-laws." We have already shown above that the major cultural categories *jñāti* and *kuṭumba* do not correspond to the categories "consanguines" and "affines." The categories *jñāti* and *kuṭumba* are present in the patterning of the kinship terminology and the categories "consanguine" and "affine" are not.

Let us begin by examining the category *jñāti*. The core of the kinship terminology consists of the eight basic terms discussed above. These are the terms used to address and refer to the persons constituting a minimal family. The pattern of this set provides the pattern for all of the many other terms used to denote particular classes of kinsmen in Bengali. In other words, all the terms for classes of *jñāti* outside the minimal family are derived from the eight basic terms. These terms are formed in a number of ways: by compounding two or more basic terms;[10] by changing the gender of a term;[11] by affixing to and/or strengthening a term;[12] and by semantic modification.[13]

According to Bengalis, the minimal family is not the only normal form of the family. Something characterized by Western social scientists as the "joint" or "extended" family—what we call the maximal family—is also regarded as normal. The persons belonging to this unit constitute the par excellence *jñāti* [14] and are distinguished in the kinship terminology from other *jñāti*. The distinction between the terms for par excellence *jñāti* and those for other *jñāti* can most conveniently be seen proceeding from higher to lower generations. Here we are primarily concerned with the standard colloquial terms, and for the present we confine ourselves to terms used by a male.

Ascending generations. In the third ascending generation only two classes of kinsmen are designated in the standard colloquial language: *po-bābā* ("father's father's father") and *jhi-mā* ("father's father's mother"), in Sanskrit *prapitāmaha* and *prapitāmahī*. Both of these are par excellence *jñāti*. The absence of special terms to designate mother's father's father and mother's father's mother is an indication of the stress placed upon a man's father's *kula* in relation to his mother's father's *kula*.[15]

In the second ascending generation, four classes of kinsmen are designated: *ṭhākur-dādā* ("father's father") and *ṭhākur-mā* ("father's mother"), par excellence *jñāti*, are clearly distinguished from *dādā-maśāy* ("mother's father") and *didi-mā* ("mother's mother").[16] The opposition between these two pairs of classes, the opposition between one's *pitṛ-kula* and one's *mātṛ-kula*, is clearly marked in the corresponding Sanskrit terms, *pitāmaha* and *pitāmahī*, vs. *mātāmaha* and *mātāmahī*, formed from the terms *pitā* ("father") and *mātā* ("mother") by adding the adjectival suffix *-maha*. However, this distinction may be collapsed by the use of the term *dādā* to refer both to father's father and mother's father and the term *dādī* to refer both to father's mother and mother's mother. Thus, at one level in the terminology the unity of these four progenitors is stressed, while at another level the distinction between one's *pitṛ-kula* and one's *mātṛ-kula*, between sharing and gift-giving, is stressed.

In the first ascending generation, apart from a man's mother and father, five classes of *jñāti* appear to be designated: *jeṭhā* ("father's elder brother"), *khuṛā*, or its alternate *kākā* ("father's younger brother"), *māmā* ("mother's brother"), *pisī* ("father's sister"), and *māsī* ("mother's sister"). On the surface this set of terms may be characterized as "bifurcate collateral" in that father's brothers are distinguished from father and from mother's brothers. Close semantic examination reveals, however, that these terms are actually "bifurcate merging," or, to put it more accurately, these terms distinguish two *kula*s, that of a man's father and that of his mother's father. *Jeṭhā* and *khuṛā* are contracted forms of *jyeṣṭha-tāta* and *khulla-tāta*, meaning "elder father" and "younger father" respectively. In Sanskrit, the identity of these two is signaled by the use of the single paternal term *pitṛvya* for both. The term *māmā*, or *mātula*,[17] by contrast, is derived not from a paternal term but from the maternal term *mā* and is best understood as meaning "maternal father." Thus, at one level the terminology groups a man's father and his brothers together and opposes them to the mother's brothers. This reflects the fact that a man's father and his brothers are par excellence *jñāti* while his mother's brothers are not.

The terms for the wives of *jeṭhā, khuṛā*, and *māmā* are derived from these terms by changing their gender from masculine to feminine: thus, *jeṭhī*, *khuṛī* (or *kākī*), and *māmī*.[18] This terminological alteration reflects a point of fundamental importance to our account of Bengali kinship, the fact that marriage transforms a woman into the half-body of her husband. Thus, just as one's mother is a par excellence *jñāti* by virtue of her marriage to one's father, so the wives of father's brothers are also par excellence *jñāti*. In other words, whenever a term is generated by changing the gender of a *jñāti* term from masculine to feminine, that term is also classed as a *jñāti* term. Thus the opposition between the *pitṛ-kula* and *mātṛ-kula* is also sustained in the terms for the wives of father's and mother's brothers.

The importance of this opposition can be seen by looking at the terms *pisī* and *māsī*.[19] Unlike the other paternal and maternal terms, these two are simply denotative terms, meaning "father's sister" and "mother's sister." With respect to *kula* these are ambiguous terms, which is appropriate since they refer to women who have married out of a man's *pitṛ-kula* and *mātṛ-kula*. Before marriage they are classed as persons of one's *pitṛ-kula* and *mātṛ-kula*, but after marriage they are not. This is particularly important with respect to a man's *pisī*, since before marriage she is classed as a par excellence *jñāti* but after marriage is not. A man's *jeṭhā, jeṭhī, khuṛā*, and *khuṛī* are unambiguously classed as paternal persons belonging to one's father's *kula*. *Māmā* and *māmī* are similarly classed as maternal persons belonging to one's mother's father's *kula*. Their *jñāti* relationship to a man does not change; the *jñāti* relationship of a man's *pisī* and *māsī*, by contrast, does change. The terms for their husbands, *pise* and *meso*, are formed by changing the gender of the term from feminine to masculine. In other words, whenever a term is generated by changing the gender of a *jñāti* term from feminine to masculine, that term is classed not as a *jñāti* term but as a *kuṭumba* term. Thus the terminology clearly distinguishes between male *jñāti* and their spouses, on the one hand, and female *jñāti* and their spouses, on the other. This opposition is intersected by another one: the paternal terms *jeṭhā, khuṛā*, and *pisī* stand in opposition to the maternal ones, *māmā* and *māsī*, without regard to sex. That is, all persons connected with the *pitṛ-kula* are "fatherly," regardless of their sex, and those connected with the *mātṛ-kula* are "motherly," regardless of their sex. Still another pattern sorts these kinsmen by sex,[20] designating all the males as paternal and all the females as maternal. This pattern is signaled by the compounding of these terms with the paternal terms *maśāy* and *bābu*[21] and the maternal term *mā*. For example, a man properly addresses and refers to his father's elder brother as *jeṭhā-maśāy* and his wife as *jeṭhī-mā*. A mother's brother may be addressed or referred to as *māmā-bābu* and her sister as *māsī-mā*.[22]

Once again, more than one pattern emerges from the kinship terminology. Three patterns may be seen in the terms for the first ascending generation: the first distinguishes both males and females of the *pitṛ-kula* from those of the *mātṛ-kula*; a second pattern distinguishes paternal from maternal persons without regard to sex; and the third pattern identifies all males as paternal and all females as maternal, regardless of *kula*.

Ego's generation. The patterning of the terms for *jñāti* in a man's own generation is somewhat different. Apart from his "own" (*nijer*) brothers and sisters, the terms *bhāi* ("brother") and *bon* ("sister") are also applied to all the children of *jñāti* of the first ascending generation, making no distinction between one's own siblings and the others.[23] However, these brothers and sisters may be distinguished from his own siblings by the use of the modifiers *jeṭhtuto-*, *khuṛtuto-* (or *kākāto-*), *māmāto-*, *pistuto-*, and *māstuto-*. The terms *bhāi* and *bon*, when combined with these modifiers, mean "brother who is the son of the elder father," and so forth.[24] As is evident, the same five classes of *jñāti* that are distinguished in the first ascending generation are also distinguished in ego's own generation. Since the same terms are used to class *jñāti* in this generation as in the preceding one, the same distinctions among *kula*s made there are also made here. Just as father and father's brothers are all classed in the terminology as "fathers" because they belong to the same *pitṛ-kula*, their sons consider each other to be the par excellence *jñāti* of the same generation. This is reflected in the use of the term *bhāi*. Often when a man speaks of his brothers he refers not only to his own brothers, the sons of his father, but also to the sons of the other fathers of his *pitṛ-kula*. Accordingly, a man's eldest brother (*baṛo bhāi*) may be the son not of his own father but of his father's brother. Once again, terminological and usage patterns both stress the unity of males of a man's *kula* in each generation.

It is at a more general level that the other three sets of *jñāti* belonging to a man's own generation are classed as siblings. The *māmāto-*, *pistuto-*, and *māstuto-bhāi/-bon* are persons of other *kula*s.[25] The unity of *jñāti* of the same generation is subordinated to the unity of *jñāti* of the same generation and of the same *kula* as well.

A man's own wife is distinguished in the terminology from his brother's wife; the general term for brother's wife combines a term for "brother" with a term for "wife," *bhāj* or *bhrātṛ-jāyā* ("brother's wife").[26] Similarly, the term for the husband of a man's sister is formed by modifying a term for "sister" with a term for husband, *bhaginī-pati* ("sister's husband"). The classification of these terms parallels the classification of the terms for spouses of *jñāti* in the preceding generation: whenever one of the terms for "wife" is compounded with a *jñāti* term, the class thus designated is also *jñāti*; by contrast, whenever a term for "husband" is compounded with a *jñāti* term the class thus designated is not *jñāti* but *kuṭumba*. This pair of rules also applies in the first and second descending generations.

Descending generations. In the first descending generation, apart from a man's own son (*chele, po*) and daughter (*meye, jhi*), four classes of *jñāti* are designated in the terminology. A man's brother's son and daughter, *bhāi-po* and *bhāi-jhi*,[27] are distinguished from his sister's son and daughter, *bhāgne*[28] and *bhāgnī*. The parallel terms to *bhāi-po/-jhi*, *bon-po/-jhi*, are used not by a man but only by a woman to refer to her sister's children. A woman does use the terms *bhāgne* and *bhāgnī*, however, to refer to her *husband's* sister's children. These asymmetries in the terminology reflect the asymmetrical relationship of a woman as half-body of her husband and stress the distinction between par excellence *jñāti* and other *jñāti*.[29]

A term for "wife," *bou*, is used to designate the wife of a man's son. It may be compounded with the terms *bhāi-po* and *bhāgne* to designate their wives. A term for "husband," *jāmāi*, designates a man's daughter's husband and, compounded with the terms *bhāi-jhi* and *bhāgnī*, designates their husbands. These compound terms designate *jñāti* and *kuṭumba* classes, respectively, according to the rule stated above: the wives of *jñāti* are classed as *jñāti*; the husbands of *jñāti* are classes as *kuṭumba*.

In the second descending generation, four classes of *jñāti* are designated in the terminology: *pautra* ("son's son"), *pautrī* ("son's daughter"), *dauhitra*[30] ("daughter's son"), and *dauhitrī* ("daughter's daughter"). Just as the distinction between father's and mother's parents may be ignored in the terminology, so too the distinction between son's and daughter's children may be ignored. Thus one pair of terms, *nāti*[31] and *nātnī*, is used to designate both son's and daughter's son and daughter. In standard colloquial language these latter terms have the par excellence meanings of son's son and daughter, once again stressing their importance as par excellence *jñāti*. The terms for the spouses of *nāti* and *nātnī* are formed by compounding these terms with the terms for "wife" and "husband"—thus, *nāt-bou* and *nāt-jāmāi*.

"Distant relations." The terms for *jñāti* distinguish three sets of persons: (1) a minimal family, (2) the persons who, when added to set one, make up a maximal family, and (3) those constituting the remainder of one's total set of *jñāti*. Thus far the categories of kinsmen designated by these three sets of terms have all been those classed as "near" (*nikaṭa, kāche*) or "own" (*nija*) in relationship (*samparke*) (referring to genealogical nearness, not some measure of love). However, there is an additional, opposed category of *jñāti* also designated by these terms, excluding set one, who are classed as "distant" or "other than" (*dūra*) in relationship. Just as the term *jñāti* is used as a modifier to distinguish close *jñāti* outside the family from the persons of one's family, so too, at this level, it may be used to distinguish distant from close *jñāti*.

For example, any *jñāti* classed as a "brother" of one's father's father is designated by the same term as father's father, *ṭhākur-dādā*; and his wife is designated by the term *ṭhākur-mā*. In the first ascending generation, any *jñāti* classed as a "brother" of one's father is designated by a term for father's brother, *jeṭhā* or *khuṛā*; his wife is termed *jeṭhī* or *khuṛī*. In one's own generation, the sons of *jñāti* classed as brothers by one's father are designated by the terms *jeṭhtuto-bhāi* or *khuṛtuto-bhāi*. (See Vatuk [1969] for a full discussion of the designation of distant kinsmen.) The same principle of classification applies in succeeding generations. The *jñāti* of this set may be distinguished from one's "near" *jñāti* by adding the modifier *dūra-samparke* ("distantly related") before the appropriate term. Still other modifiers are used to generate classes of one's own people (*ātmīya-svajana*) who are not *jñāti* or *kuṭumba*. Examples of such modifiers are *guru*, as in *guru-bhāi*, "brother in respect of a common *guru*," or *guru-mā*, "mother who is the wife of my *guru*"; and *dharma*, as *dharma-bon*, "sister in respect of common worship."

Terms for Kuṭumba

Terms for classes of kinsmen who are only *kuṭumba* and not *jñāti*, such as *pise*, *meso*, *bhaginī-pati*, *jāmāi*, and *nāt-jāmāi*, are all formed by modifying *jñāti* forms. The classes of kinsmen designated by these terms are all receivers of daughters (*kanyā*) and other gifts in relation to a man; they collectively constitute the set of a man's *jāmāi*s. A man's *jāmāi*s constitute one set of his par excellence *kuṭumba*, the receivers of daughters; the other set of par excellence *kuṭumba* consists of givers of daughters. This latter set of kinsmen is designated by terms that are semantically but not etymologically derivable from the eight basic terms; these are the terms *śvaśura*, "wife's father" (also used by a woman to refer to her husband's father, see p. 82), best rendered in English as "marital father," and *śālā*, "wife's brother." Like the terms for *jñāti*, these two terms are, of course, modified to produce terms designating other classes of *kuṭumba*, which are listed in table 4.

Since a man is not considered a whole person without a wife, his wife's father is considered, in a sense, to be his father. Hence, *śvaśura* is semantically equivalent to "father" (and he is conventionally listed as one of a man's "five fathers") and *śālā* to "brother"; indeed, a man commonly addresses his wife's father as *bābā* and his wife's brother, if he is older, as *dādā* or, if he is younger, by name, just as he would his own brother. Similarly, the wife's mother, *śāśuṛī*, is addressed as *mā*, and the wife's sister, *śālī*, if she is older, as *didi*. Yet he never addresses his own father as *śvaśura* or his brother as *śālā*—to do so would be extremely insulting. Application of the terms *śvaśura* and *śālā* to persons who do not belong to those particular classes has a meaning approximately equivalent to: "I am intimate with your daughter or sister." Both the restriction on the uses of these special *kuṭumba* terms and the common use of *jñāti* terms to address persons belonging to these classes suggests the heavy emphasis placed upon sharing relationships in Bengali culture. The use of the term *kuṭum* or *sammandhi* to designate a wife's brother, especially a wife's elder brother, stresses his role as a man's par excellence gift-giving relative. Even though the gifts coming from a man's wife's father's house may originate with his *śvaśura* or even his *śvaśura*'s father, it is inevitably the *śālā* who comes bearing them.

Three other terms in this set are of some interest: *bhāyrā-bhāi*, *behāi*, and *tāoi*. The term *bhāyrā-bhāi*, "wife's sister's husband," unlike the others of this set, is derived from one of the eight basic terms, *bhāi* ("brother"). This term seems to imply that he is not related by the gift of a daughter as are other persons in this set, and this is correct. Consistent with the Bengali conception of marriage, he is not incorporated into a man's wife's father's *kula*; rather, a man's *śvaśura*'s daughter (i.e., wife's sister) is incorporated into the *kula* of the *bhāyrā-bhāi*. Hence both one's self and his *bhāyrā-bhāi* are related in the same way to the same *śvaśura*; both have accepted daughters from him. As we have seen, there are two complementary and opposed modes of relationship, relations of sharing and of gift-giving. Since *bhāyrā-bhāi*s are not related to one another by giving (or acceptance), they must be related by sharing, and this is how the relationship is conceived in Bengali culture. They are related in that they share the same *śvaśura*, who, it will be remembered, is classed as a "father," so they must then, be brothers. Obviously, one's *bhāyrā-bhāi* does not share the same food, house, property, and so on, as does one's own brother; in many respects it is a kind of null sharing relationship. This distinction is maintained by the use of the modifier *bhāyrā-* before the term for "brother."

According to the usual criteria, *behāi*, "child's spouse's father," and the feminine form *behān*, would not be considered "kinship terms." Derived from the Sanskrit word *vaivāhika*, *behāi* means "maker of a marriage." *Behāi* and *behān* are not regarded as par excellence *kuṭumba*s because their relationship of gift and acceptance is only indirect, through their children's marriage, rather than directly with respect to one another. The terms *tāoi*, "sibling's spouse's father," and *māoi*, "sibling's spouse's mother," uncertainly derived from the Sanskrit word for marriage modified by terms for "father" and "mother," also designate classes of indirect gift-giving relatives.

The Female Ego

The patterning in the kinship terminology obviously differs in some important respects when ego is a female rather than a male. With two exceptions, one minor and one major, an unmarried female designates her kinsmen by the same terms used by her brothers. She designates her brother's wives as *bhāj* regardless of their ages. The terms she uses makes no distinction of *kula* between children of her brothers (*bhāi-po/-jhi*) and of her sisters (*bon-po/-jhi*), reflecting the fact that neither of these belong to her *kula* after she is married. The terms her brother uses to designate his sister's son and daughter (*bhāgne*, *bhāgnī*) are used by a married woman to designate her husband's sister's children, emphasizing the fact that she becomes a *jñāti* of her husband and, thereby, of his sister and her children, while a man does not become *jñāti* to his wife's sister or her children.

When a woman is married, generally speaking, she may address her husband's relatives by the same terms that her husband uses, just as a man may address his wife's relatives by the same terms she uses. And, just as a man may use a special set of terms to designate his wife's relatives, so too may a woman. In the first and second ascending generations, the term *śvaśura* and its derivatives may be used to designate her husband's father, father's father, mother, and so forth, just as a man uses them to designate his wife's father, and so forth. In her own generation, however, the terms a female uses for her husband's siblings and their spouses differ from the terms a man uses for his wife's siblings and their spouses. These terms are: *bhāśur* ("husband's elder brother"), *deor* ("husband's younger brother"), *jā* ("husband's brother's wife"), *nanod* ("husband's sister"), and *nandāi* ("husband's sister's husband"). The term *bhāśur* is derived from a compound of the Sanskrit words *bhrātṛ* ("brother") and *śvaśura* and means "*śvaśura* who is a brother."[32] Of unclear derivation, the term *deor*, or its *tatsama* equivalent *devara*, is used in Sanskrit to designate all of one's husband's brothers.[33] The term *jā* is derived from the Sanskrit word *yātā*, meaning "she who goes," possibly a reference to her going away to her father's house, thus leaving ego in peace. The term *nanod*, derived from the Sanskrit *nanandā*, means roughly "she who is not pleased." In the first descending generation, a woman uses the terms *bhāśur-po/-jhi*, *deor-po/-jhi*, and *bhāgne/bhāgnī* to designate her husband's sibling's children and distinguish them from her own.

The failure of North Indian terminologies to distinguish all of a man's wife's relatives from all of a woman's husband's relatives, given the fact that these two sets of kinsmen are classed differently and have contrasting codes for conduct, has been seen as an "inconsistency" by at least one anthropologist.[34] However, this is not really a problem. From the genealogical perspective, as conceived in Bengali culture and probably in North India generally, the same terms have the same meanings for both men and women. From the perspective of *kula* and code for conduct, the meanings of these terms for male and female ego are so radically opposed to one another that (with one possible exception)[35] there is little chance of any confusion between them. When a person hears a man refer to his *śvaśura*, he presumes that the man is referring to a *kuṭumba* relationship and gift-giving code for conduct. By contrast, when a woman refers to her *śvaśura*, the presumption is that she is referring to a *jñāti* relationship and a sharing code for conduct.

That a man and his wife have different terms for one another's siblings is also of little consequence. We have already seen that the greatest degree of terminological differentiation occurs in ego's own generation and that differences between contrasting sets of relatives may be collapsed in ascending and descending generations. Both of these features operate with respect to a spouse's relatives. For example, the term *ṭhākur*, "lord," or, more accurately, "embodied deity," and its female forms *ṭhākurānī*, *ṭhākrun*, *ṭhān*, may be used by a married woman, in conjunction with other kinship terms, to designate her husband's relatives. Since these terms are not used by a married man, they do distinguish between the one set of relatives and the other. On the other hand, the distinction between the two sets of spouses' brothers may be collapsed, for both may be referred to as *śvaśurya*.

Summary

Our analysis of Bengali kinship terminology has departed from previous analyses of North Indian terminologies, all of which have been based upon the assumption that the underlying pattern somehow reflects the distinction between "consanguines" and "affines." Since these are not the basic categories of kin in Bengali or North Indian culture, none of these earlier analyses has been completely successful in showing the patterns that are imbedded in the terminology. Bengalis regard as their par excellence kinsmen persons with whom they "share the same body," *jñāti* or *sapiṇḍa* relations. The feature which makes this category different from the consanguine or "blood relative" category is that a number of "affinal" relationships are substantialized and included in it. One consequence of this cultural conception is that all families are thought to be units of shared bodily substance rather than conglomerates of affinity and consanguinity defined by law.

The basic pattern in the terminology that our analysis has revealed is contained in the terms for classes of *jñāti* composing the minimal family and its variants. The core of the kinship terminology consists of eight basic terms which designate the classes of kin in the minimal family and provide a complete paradigm for the patterning of all the other kinship terms. The persons in the minimal family are distinguished from all other kinsmen, who are designated by modified forms of the eight basic terms. The terminology as a whole makes two kinds of distinctions: on the one hand, it distinguishes classes of kinsmen in the normal family from those in abnormal families, and, on the other hand, it distinguishes classes of kinsmen in the minimal family from those in other families. The next level, the maximal family, which encompasses the minimal family, is terminologically distinguished from all other categories of *jñāti*, such as the mother's father's *kula*, which may also be classed as *kuṭumba*. The fact that the terms for the set of overlapping *jñāti* and *kuṭumba* are derived from the eight basic terms for *jñāti* and not from the etymologically different terms for par excellence *kuṭumba* reflects the primary stress placed upon the shared bodily substance and the sharing code for conduct that define a family. At a third level, close *jñāti* of all categories are distinguished from distant *jñāti*. Finally, at the highest level, *jñāti*, sharing relatives, are distinguished from par excellence *kuṭumba*, gift-giving (or receiving) relatives.

One other feature of the terminology is that it provides for two apparently contradictory types of kin classification; it is at the same time both "individualizing" and "collectivizing." Any kinsmen may be designated by a term that distinguishes him from all others or, with equal facility, designated by a term that classes him in one of the eight basic relationships. Normally, Bengalis subordinate the analytical or descriptive capacity of the terminology to its synthesizing or classificatory capacity, which is a reflection of the primary importance they place upon subordinating smaller collectivities and individuals to the larger ones of maximal family, clan, and community. This tendency extends beyond the *jñāti-kuṭumba* category to include persons with whom one has very diverse kinds of relationships and to reach the limits of solidary social relationships of all kinds.

Conclusion

We have sought to understand Bengali "kinship" as a cultural system—that is, as a system of symbols shared by Bengalis rather than as a system of concrete groups or behaviors. Our earlier efforts to discover principles of a Bengali kinship system in masses of census and genealogical data yielded many interesting facts but no principles by which these facts could be understood as a system. Differences between Bengali and American kinship were clear, but we could characterize them only in terms of "the joint family system," "patrilineality," the "facts" of biological relationship, and other superficially apparent distinctions. It was only when we began to investigate the codes for conduct governing action rather than specific acts, and the defining features of groups and relationships rather than the groups and relationships themselves that the principles we sought began to emerge.

It may appear that we have reified a single set of "ideal" constructs from a heterogeneous set of cultural data. Our experience in Bengali society has left us well aware of the diversity in the norms of kinship among Bengali Hindus, as between high, middle, and low castes, East and West Bengal, rural and urban, educated and uneducated, rich and poor, and so forth. Yet our investigation has convinced us that there is an integrated set of cultural premises and definitions that inform the patterns of classification and action of Bengalis as kinsmen.

The most fundamental question for an investigation of this kind is whether there is in Bengali culture something resembling a domain of "kinship." It is quite possible that a people might not distinguish a kinship domain from other domains of actions and relationships. What we discovered is that there is something like a domain of kinship in Bengali culture but it is different from our own. First of all, there is the category *ātmīya-svajana*, which may include practically anyone as "one's own person." Within this indefinite category there is a smaller definite category identified by the compound term *jñāti-kuṭumba*.

The next question is, How are the domains denoted by these terms defined? Here we employ the concept of "defining feature," that is, the irreducible element or set of elements that decisively distinguish one domain from all others. The term *ātmīya-svajana* denotes a domain of relationships that appears to be defined by an amorphous, heterogeneous set of features. Let us review these features, beginning first with the *jñāti-kuṭumba* category.

The defining feature of the *jñāti-kuṭumba* category of one's own people is the body or bodily substance. The *jñāti* class is defined by a shared body while the *kuṭumba* class is defined by a body given or accepted in marriage. Each of these classes is further divided into a "restricted," par excellence set and a residual set. The par excellence sets of *jñāti* and *kuṭumba* are "restricted" in the sense that they are defined either by shared or given bodily substance alone. The residual sets are marked by both—by the presence of given bodily substances in the case of *jñāti* and of shared bodily substance in the case of *kuṭumba*.

The features that define the categories of one's own people are not drawn from two contrasting orders. The two opposed features that define American kinship—"blood," a natural substance, and "law," a code for conduct—are drawn from the dualistically conceived orders of "nature" and of "law" or "morality" in American culture. We have referred to the features that define the *jñāti* and *kuṭumba* classes as "shared body" and "given or accepted body" because there is no absolute opposition between natural substance and code for conduct in Bengali culture. Bengali culture postulates a single, nondualistically conceived order of substances each of which possesses its own inherent code for conduct. Thus, the shared body that defines the *jñāti* class of relationships is a substance containing an inherent code for conduct enjoining sharing. Similarly, the given or accepted body that defines the *kuṭumba* class of relationships is a substance containing an inherent code for conduct enjoining gift-giving. One apparent implication of this monistic world view is that oppositions between coded substances can invariably be resolved into a single coded substance. Both shared body and given body, as coded substances, are resolvable into a single coded substance, the body, containing a single code for conduct that enjoins love.

The body, whether shared or given, is the defining feature of the *jñāti-kuṭumba* class of relationships. It is also the distinctive source of the love that *jñāti-kuṭumba* have for one another. Love, conceived of as a subtle essence (*rasa*), may be either egalitarian or hierarchical. While Bengalis have valued egalitarian love relationships, the predominant stress in Bengali culture has been placed on the hierarchical form of love. The combination of "hierarchy" and "love" seems contradictory from the perspective of our own culture. We stress sameness, equality, and mutuality as necessary for love and unity, and we see differences as divisive and inharmonious with proper love relationships. However, in Bengali culture it is egalitarian love that is seen as divisive. For example, the egalitarian conjugal love of husband and wife unites them to one another, but it divides the husband from his brothers and divides both husband and wife from his parents. On the other hand, the hierarchical filial love that a wife has for her husband is seen as fully harmonious with the filial love that all juniors have for their elders and therefore as uniting. Whence the "strange" notion that unity among *jñāti-kuṭumba* is achieved and sustained by the subordination of egalitarian love to hierarchical love.

Unity in the Bengali family is derived from the particular stress placed on one hierarchical love relationship. The par excellence *jñāti* of a person are also his par excellence kinsmen; they are the persons of the same family, "dependents" (*parivāra*) of the same single living "actor" or "master" (*kartā*). It is the parental love (*sneha*) of the divine *kartā* for all of his worshipful dependents—his wife, sons, sons' wives and children—and their filial love (*bhakti*) for him that unite the family and bring about its well-being (*maṅgala*). One meaning of the word *sneha* is "oil"; one meaning of *bhakti* is "to share." The Bengali Hindu image of the family is thus one of a microcosm cared for by a living deity pouring down auspicious oil that is shared in by all who depend upon him.

Love is not commonly discussed in anthropological analyses of Indian kinship systems; rather, it is authority, rights and duties, land, inheritance, the distribution of resources within the joint family, prestations, reproduction, and so forth, that are usually considered to be the essential stuff of kinship. It is certainly true that these are matters of great concern to Bengalis and that they frequently lead to conflicts, quarrels, and separation. Anyone who has watched a Bengali nurse an inheritance dispute through the courts can testify to this. These are matters that seriously affect the unity and prosperity of *jñāti-kuṭumba* in general and the Bengali family in particular. Our study of Bengali kinship as a cultural system, however, tells us about something quite different: it tells us what unites *jñāti-kuṭumba* and what holds together the family—and that is love. To translate this into the jargon of social science, love is the "independent variable" in the Bengali kinship system; property, control of resources, duties, and so on, are "dependent variables." If kinsmen have the proper kind of love for one another then they will enjoy well-being and they will not be divided by greed, selfishness, or envy.

Let us now return to the question of the larger *ātmīya-svajana* class to which the *jñāti-kuṭumba* class belongs. The *ātmīya-svajana* class, like the *jñāti-kuṭumba* class, is organized into par excellence and residual categories. In its par excellence and restricted sense, the term *ātmīya-svajana* refers to the *jñāti-kuṭumba* class. The other *ātmīya-svajana* form a residual category for which there is, as usual, no distinctive name in Bengali. As we have seen, the defining feature of the *jñāti-kuṭumba* class is the body or bodily substances coded for love and well-being. If this is the defining feature of the par excellence *ātmīya-svajana* class, then perhaps it is any substance coded for love and well-being that is the defining feature of the whole class.

Persons who are related by bodily substance are also related by nonbodily substances. Persons related by shared bodily substance, *jñāti*, are also related by the sharing of other substances conducive to prosperity, such as food, wealth, and land. Similarly, persons related by giving and receiving bodily substance, *kuṭumba*, are also related by the gift and acceptance of such nonbodily substances. Those *ātmīya-svajana* not related by bodily substance are related by nonbodily "substances" such as words, land, and food; of these, food is the most general if not the most important. As we said earlier, this residual set of one's own people is indefinite and open-ended; we can only illustrate such relationships. Of major importance in this residual category are persons said to be related by the village (*grāma-samparka*) or by the neighborhood (*pāṛā-samparka*). Persons related by initiation (*dīkṣā*), that is, by receiving powerful words (*mantra*) from the same preceptor (*guru*), are "preceptor-brothers" (*guru-bhāi*). Note that such persons as servants (*cākar*) and priests (*purohita*), even though they may be of different castes, also belong to the residual *ātmīya-svajana* class. To describe any of the persons of the *ātmīya-svajana* class as "fictive kin" does violence to Bengalis' monistic world view, for the feature that defines their relationship in Bengali culture is in fact the same as the feature that defines the *jñāti-kuṭumba* class—shared or given substance coded for love and well-being.

Both the unrestricted *ātmīya-svajana* and the restricted *jñāti-kuṭumba* classes of persons are characterized by the overlapping of categories. Some of a person's *ātmīya-svajana*—and the ones considered most important—are also classed as *jñāti-kuṭumba*. Some of a person's *jñāti* are also classed as *kuṭumba* and vice versa. These overlapping categories are a reflection of the fact that in Bengali culture what appears as an opposition at one level of thought and analysis may be resolved into a unity at another. For example, the foremost relationship created by birth, that between parents and child, is stated to be a relationship of giving and receiving in which the parents together are said to "give birth" (*janma-dāna karā*) to their child, who "receives birth" (*janma-grahaṇa karā*). However, at a higher and more general level of thought, the relationship between parents and child is said to be that of a "shared body" (*sapiṇḍa, eka-deha*). Bengali and other Indian cultural systems are thus quite different from American and Western European cultures, in which oppositions stand as fundamentally irresoluble. Our own cultural system of kinship posits "blood relatives" and "relatives by marriage" or "in-laws"—the consanguines and affines of anthropology—as wholly different and opposed classes of kinsmen. Anthropologists have coined the expression "fictive kin" to describe those persons who treat one another as kinsfolk but who are related by neither blood nor marriage, comparable to the "residual" *ātmīya-svajana* of the Bengalis. One might argue that, at least, all three classes—consanguines, affines, and fictive kin—belong to the encompassing class of "kinsmen" or "relatives." However, because of the basic dualistic assumption in our own culture, we emphasize the distinction within the larger class between persons related by natural substance and the others who are "merely" related by a code for conduct. Under the monistic postulate of Bengali culture, by contrast, all of one's own people are seen as related both by substance and by a code for conduct.

The Bengali terms for particular classes of one's own people—the "Bengali kinship terminology" as anthropologists say—are an example of the North Indian terminological systems that have been quite refractory to previous analytic efforts. The principal difficulty for most of these earlier attempts lay in the assumption that there is a single pattern organizing all the terms. In fact, Bengali terms for kinsmen are semantic compounds; they convey meanings relevant to several different contexts and systems of classification, such as sex, age, and generation, at the same time that they speak of birth and shared or exchanged body relationships. Thus, just as the classes of kinsmen overlap one another, so too the classes of terms for kinsmen overlap, representing the intersection of different contexts and systems of classification.

The Bengali "kinship terminology" includes more than two hundred lexemes. All of the Sanskrit kinship vocabulary is included in Bengali, explaining part of the unusual size of the list. However, the richness of this lexicon is principally a reflection of the fact that it provides for any kinsman to be designated by a term that distinguishes him from all others—an extreme development of descriptive terminology. Beneath this proliferation there is an equally peculiar simplicity, for all of the terms are derived from words designating the eight basic classes of kin: father, mother, son, daughter, husband, wife, brother, and sister. There are synonyms and alternate terms for each of these eight classes, and they are used to generate the descriptive terms by a variety of forms of modification, including gender change, affixing, strengthening, semantic alteration, compounding with one another, and compounding with "nonkinship" words indicating age, generation, and so forth. Although the fully elaborated descriptive terminology is known and used by all Bengalis, it is employed only in special contexts. The ordinary usage pattern assimilates all kinsmen into the eight basic classes, the persons of a minimal family, one's closest bodily relations, the par excellence *jñāti*. This tendency, which we have termed "collectivizing," as opposed to the "individualizing" tendency of the descriptive terminology, is consistent with the relative importance of collectivities in Bengali culture.

The descriptive terminology provides a man with a set of terms that distinguish the *kuṭumba*s he acquires at marriage from his *jñāti*s. These terms for his foremost *kuṭumba*s, his *śvaśura*, "wife's father," and *śālā*, "wife's brother," are etymologically unconnected with the terms for the eight basic classes of kin. However, Bengalis consider these terms as semantically derived from "father" and "brother," respectively, and they are normally so addressed. In other words, in many contexts the *kuṭumba* relationship is assimilated to the *jñāti* relationship, consistent with the relative importance of shared over given or accepted body relationships in Bengali culture. The situation of a married woman is different from that of a man: marriage creates *kuṭumba* relationships for a man where it creates *jñāti* relationships for a woman. The descriptive terminology provides a woman with a vocabulary that distinguishes all the *jñāti* she acquires through her husband from the persons who were her *jñāti* before marriage. However, in general, a woman uses all the same terms as her husband to address her *jñāti*, indicating her preeminent status as "half-body" of her husband. Overall, then, the usage pattern of the Bengali kinship terminology places greater weight upon bodily than nonbodily relationships, and upon shared rather than given and accepted bodily relationships.

The body is the central symbol of "kinship" in Bengali culture. However, it is not thought to be a static and unchanging thing; rather, it is continuously transformed and refined through life by a series of *symbolic actions*. These actions, known as *saṃskāra*s, are the "life cycle rites" of anthropology; they translate a person from one well-defined status to another one by means of a symbolic passage. They are comparable to the sacraments of Christianity except that they are thought to operate on the whole body of a person, not only on a "spiritual" or "moral" portion. Although there is considerable variation in both the beliefs and practices connected with *saṃskāra*s among Bengali Hindus, most agree that a complete cycle consists of ten rites. Each ritual has distinguishing characteristics, but underlying all of them is a single paradigmatic action, birth. Birth, in the sense of passage out of a woman's womb and into the world, is thought to be the way a person obtains his body. Thus, birth stands as the central symbolic act in Bengali kinship, just as sexual intercourse stands as the central symbolic act in American kinship (see Schneider 1968, pp. 30–54). And, like sexual intercourse in the American symbolic universe, birth symbolism in Bengal is suppressed; it is a latent paradigm for many other symbolic actions, suspended between inexpressible sanctity and repressible physiological grossness. Each of the *saṃskāra*s is an overt act of birth in a symbolic disguise.

Marriage is invariably the first *saṃskāra* in every Bengali list, even though it is the last to come in life. It is usually the most elaborate of the *saṃskāra*s and has a structure that moves between heavy, formal Vedic rituals conducted by men and the light, informal "popular" "women's rites" which are marked by joking about the prospective sexual relationship of the couple. Marriage involves a rebirth for both husband and wife. Before marriage a man's body is thought to be incomplete; he is not qualified to make offerings to the deities for this reason. At the time of marriage he passes to the "householder" stage of life and is reborn as a complete and autonomous man. At the same time, his wife is reborn with him as his "half-body." She was previously a person of her father's family and clan; marriage makes her into a person of her husband's family and clan. Marriage culminates in the union of husband and wife for the purpose of procreating a son, and thus begins a new cycle of *saṃskāra*s.

The shared body relationships that are created by birth are transformed by death, and there is a cycle of rites to be performed for the dead body that give it rebirth. When a father dies, it is the duty of his son to burn his gross body, thus liberating his subtle body. The son, who was nourished and cared for by his father in life, is to nourish and care for his father in death. In a series of offerings called *śrāddha*s the son faithfully honors and feeds the subtle body of his deceased father until he is able to join with his ancestors. The living body of a man and the love that he shares out equally to his dependents are regarded by Bengalis as the sources of the unity of the family. When that man dies, the sources of unity are taken away and it is thought proper for his sons to divide their families from one another. When it is properly carried out, the division of a family protects and fosters the unity of the clan, spreading the net of solidary relationships ever wider in each generation.

At the beginning of this study we affected agnosticism on the question of what "kinship" might mean in Bengali culture, since we had no right to assume that any such category exists. Yet we have often written as if we were quite confident of our subject matter and sure that we were dealing with a clearly delimited domain in Bengali culture. Before concluding it is worth looking back again briefly to see what it is we have examined. Our sources, whether they were living villagers or ancient literary works, were unanimous in the belief that Bengalis have "relationships" (*samparka*) with one another. Foremost among these are the relationships of *jñāti*, a category which, while it is not defined in the same way as "consanguines" in our own kinship system, seems to stand in an analogous position. In addition to the *jñāti* there are *kuṭumba*, again defined differently but analogous to our "affines." But beyond these two categories lay the heterogeneous and amorphous category of "one's own people" who were neither *jñāti* nor *kuṭumba*. We discovered how this category was defined. We did not ask, however, "Is that all?" We did not ask if anyone is excluded from this so-called kinship system. We had better answer this question before we finish—the answer is yes. Beyond the pale of one's own people there are all manner of shopkeepers, policemen, rickshaw pullers, absentee landlords, wandering beggars, railway clerks, government servants, and strangers with whom one may have an encounter without having a relationship. Modes of interaction vary from extremely formal to extremely informal and, more often than not, involve the use of a "kinship term" or two. But when a Bengali is asked whether he has a "relationship" with such a person—"Is he one of your own people?"—the answer is an indubitable no. So "kinship" for Bengalis does have boundaries, even if they are a bit fuzzy. Where the Bengali conception of one's own people differs from the American notion of kinship is in the desire to reach out to include all with whom one has personal connections—to include the widest possible range of what we lamely call "solidary relationships."

An Indigenous Account of Kinship

Appendix 1

The short description given below is a translation from the Sanskrit of a portion of a chapter from the *Brahmavaivarta Purāṇa* (1.10.138–370; this translation is based on two versions of the text, *Purāṇas* [1909] and that contained in *Śabdakalpadrumaḥ* [s.v. *sambandha*]). This collection of "old traditions" (*purāṇa*) appears to be a text that was compiled and modified in the Bengal region over a long period of time, beginning in the tenth century and ending in the sixteenth (see Hazra 1940, p. 250). Apart from its intrinsic interest, the account is worthy of attention because we found it after we had done much of our research and reached many of our conclusions. It is for this reason that we include it in an appendix rather than in the main body of our work.

The major term used in the account to denote a relationship is the term *sambandha*, which means, literally, "tying (or binding) together." Though used differently elsewhere (see p. 16), it is used here to distinguish a domain of solidarity or "kinship" relationships. The definitions of *sambandha* relationships supplied by this treatise, while all very brief, are of course of great interest. The text distinguishes three kinds of *sambandha*s—*yonija*, *vidyāja*, and *prītija*. The term *yoni* has a number of meanings. It can denote, among other things, uterus or the vulva—that is, the female reproductive organs. More generally, however, it can be used to refer to any place or source of birth or origin. It is in this more abstract sense that the term is used here. Thus the compound term *yonija* might best be rendered as "born of (*ja*) the human reproductive organs or substances (*yoni*)." In other words, one type of *sambandha* or solidary relationship is that defined by birth and the human body. The other two types of relationships are those born of "knowledge" (*vidyā*) and "love" (*prīti*). We shall return to these later.

It is clear from the way the treatise proceeds that the first definition refers to those relationships classed by Bengalis as *jñāti-kuṭumba* relationships. The text does not use this specific compound term; in fact, it does not use the word *kuṭumba* at all. It does employ the term *jñāti*, but it does so to refer to the class of those persons beginning with the sons of a brother's sons. On first sight this appears to be a very different use of the word *jñāti* from the one we have reported for Bengali Hindus. This seems to be confirmed by the contrast implied between the term *jñāti* and the term *kula-jāta*, which is used to refer to the class of persons beginning with the son of one's son's son's son.

These difficulties are easily resolved. As we have shown elsewhere (pp. 14–15), the term *jñāti* is often employed to denote persons of the same clan and especially "brothers" or "cousins" who are more distantly related—that is, persons for whom there are no specific kinship terms. This is precisely the way the term is used here. Similarly, the term *kula-jāta* is used to refer to distantly related "sons" for whom there are no specific terms. As for the distinction made between *jñāti* and *kula-jāta*, it is noteworthy but not fundamental. The term *kula-jāta* means "born of the same clan" or, in physiological terms, born of the semen or seed of the same ancestral male. In this general sense both of the classes distinguished in the *Purāṇa* are *kula-jāta*. All that the text has done is to make a distinction between two complementary subclasses; distantly related "brothers" of the same clan, and distantly related (in fact, as yet unborn) "sons." Thus, the terms *jñāti* and *kula-jāta* are used in the account below in a restricted sense to refer to persons of the same clan (sharing relatives) who are more distantly related and for whom there are no specific terms. However, there can be no doubt that both of these terms in a more general sense denote the same class of persons for the compilers of the *Purāṇa* as does the term *jñāti* for modern Bengalis.

The class of relationships denoted by the term *bāndhava* in the account below appears to be the same as that denoted by the term *kuṭumba* in Bengali, though again, as in the case of the term *jñāti*, it is used to refer to those members of the *bāndhava* or *kuṭumba* class, gift-giving relatives, for whom no specific terms are given. As pointed out elsewhere (pp. 117–18, n. 4), the term *bāndhava* is used in those places where Bengali sources or speakers would employ the term *kuṭumba*.

The term *vidyāja*, "born of knowledge" apparently refers to the relationships one has with his *guru* or teacher and, through his body, with his wife, son, and daughter. The term *prītija*, "born of love," is used to denote the relationship one has with a "friend" (*mitra*). Note, however, that these are mentioned in the *Purāṇa* in connection with *bāndhava* or gift-giving relationships and not *jñāti* or sharing relationships. Other relationships mentioned in the lists of "mothers" and "fathers"—those of master, master's wife, savior, and the like—could also be taken to refer to other persons with whom one has solidary gift and acceptance relationships but who are not related by bodily substance. Thus, it is clear that the *Purāṇa* uses the term *sambandha* to refer in its broadest sense to solidary relationships above and beyond those characterized by a bodily relationship. In other words, the class of relationships denoted by the term *sambandha* is largely coterminous with the class of relations designated by the term *ātmīya-svajana*, "one's own people."

A Treatise on Relationships [*Sambandha-nirṇaya*]

I shall tell you of the relationship [*sambandha*] of the one with the other as declared in the Veda and proclaimed by Brahmā for all occupational castes [*jāti*] everywhere. He who is related as giver of birth [*janma-dātā*] is father [*pitā, tāta, janaka*]. She who gives birth [*prasūr*] in her womb [*garbha*] is mother [*ambā, mātā, jananī*]. *Pitāmaha* is father's father; his father is *prapitāmaha*; and *jñāti* [sharing relatives] above and beyond him are called *sagotra* [of the same clan]. *Mātāmaha* is mother's father and *pramātāmaha* is the father of *mātāmaha*, and his father is the one known as *vṛddha* [old]. *Pitāmahī* is the father's mother, and her husband's mother is *prapitāmahī*. *Mātāmahī* is mother's mother and is to be worshiped like one's own mother. *Pramātāmahī* is known as the wife of *pramātāmaha* and *vṛddha-pramātāmahī* is known as his father's wife.

Father's brother is *pitṛvya* and mother's brother is *mātula*. Father's sister is *pitur-bhagnī* and mother's sister is *māsurī*.

The one born [*janya*] as a male [*puṃ*] is denominated the *sūnu* [son], *tanaya* [the one who perpetuates one's coded bodily substance by accepting birth], *putra* [he who saves one from hell], *āt-*

maja [born from one's self], *dāyāda* [he who receives the paternal wealth], and *dhana-bhāk* [sharer of wealth], *vīrya-ja* [born of one's semen]. The one born as a female is proclaimed the *duhitā* [daughter] and *kanyā* [she who desires a husband]. The wife of a son is known as *vadhū* and husband of a daughter as *jāmātā*.

The husband [*kānta*, the desired one] is related as a *pati* [master], *priya* [beloved one], *bhartā* [supporter], and *svāmī* [lord]. Wife's brother is *śyālaka* and wife's sister is *śyālikā*. *Devara* is the husband's brother and *nanandā* the husband's sister. *Śvaśura* is the father of the husband and *śvaśrū* is the mother of the husband.

The *patnī* [wife] is related as a *bhāryā* [she who is to be supported], *jāyā* [child-bearer], *priyā* [beloved one], *kāntā* [desired one], and *strī* [woman]. Wife's mother is *śvaśrū*, while her father is remembered as *śvaśura*.

He born of the same womb [*sagarbha*] and co-uterine [*sodara*] is remembered as *bhrātā* [brother] and she of the same womb as *bhaginī* [sister]. Sister's son is *bhāgineya* and brother's son is *bhrātṛ-ja* [born of the brother]. The *śyāla* [wife's brother] is a brother because his *bhaginī-pati* [sister's husband] is also his sister's desired one [*bhaginī-kānta*]; so too is *śyālī-pati* [wife's sister husband], in this case by virtue of having the same marital father [*śvaśura*].

Śvaśura [spouse's father] is also known as father [*pitā*], the equivalent of his own father, his giver of birth [*janma-dātā*]. Among men they count five—the master, giver of food [*anna-dātā*]; the savior, deliverer from fear [*bhaya-trātā*]; the father of one's wife; the teacher, giver of knowledge [*vidyā-dātā*]; and, the genitor, giver of birth [*janma-dātā*]—as fathers.

The wife [*bhāryā*] and sister [*bhaginī*] of one's master [*anna-dātā*], the teacher's wife [*guru-kāminī*]; mother and her co-wife [*sapatnī*]; one's daughter [*kanyā*] together with the son's wife [*putra-priyā*]; mother's mother; father's mother; wife's mother; father's and mother's sisters; father's brother's wife [*pitṛvyāṇī*]; and, mother's brother's wife [*mātulānī*] are the fourteen mothers.

They call the son's son *pautra* and his son *prapautra*; the *vaṃśa* [clan offspring] beginning with his son they class as *kula-jātas* [sharing relatives, those born of the clan]. On the other hand, the son of one's daughter is one's *dauhitra* and those beginning with his sons are *bāndhavas* [gift-giving relatives, those to whom one is tied]. Likewise, men beginning with the son of a sister's son are remembered as *bāndhavas*, while those beginning with the sons of a brother's sons are, again, remembered as *jñāti* [sharing relatives].

The brother who is the teacher's son [*guru-putra*] is to be cared for [*poṣya*] as a prime [*parama*] *bāndhava* [relative by gift and acceptance]; and the sister who is the teacher's daughter [*guru-kanyā*] is to be cared for like a mother. And the brother who is an elder related through one's son is to be cared for as a well-loved [*susnigdha*] *bāndhava*. The brother who is marital father of one's son and a *bandhu* [gift-giving relative] is remembered as a *vaivāhika* [marriage maker]. The marital father of one's daughter is also declared to have that relationship [*sambandha*]. And the men who are elders related through one's married daughter are also remembered as *bāndhava*s. The expression "men are remembered as *bāndhava*s," has thus in some contexts the additional meaning of "brothers, namely well-loved [*susnigdha*] *bāndhava*s [giving and receiving relatives]." An elder related through a brother who is a marital father is worshiped like one's own elder.

Him with whom one has a relationship [*bandhutā*] apart from these is called a friend [*mitra*]. A friend is known as a giver of well-being [*sukha-prada*], while a giver of distress [*duḥkha-da*] is called an enemy [*ripu*]. As the gods would have it [*daivāt*], a relative [*bāndhava*] may be a giver of distress while one who has no bodily relationship [*niḥsambandhī*] may be a giver of well-being. O best of Brahmans, the relationships [*sambandha*] of men are said to be of three kinds on earth—born of knowledge [*vidyāja*], born of the body/reproductive organs [*yonija*], and born of love [*prītija*]. A friend is known to be born of love; that relationship is indeed difficult to obtain.

Bengali Muslim Kinship

Appendix 2

With one important exception, the kinship categories of Bengali Muslims appear to be the same as those of Bengali Hindus. The categories of *ātmīya-svajana* and *jñāti-kuṭumba* are structured in the same way for Muslims and Hindus. *Jñāti* relationships are sharing relationships; *kuṭumbas* follow a gift-giving code for conduct. Birth is the central act and defining feature of kinship for Muslims, as it is for Hindus. Even though Muslim marriage is generally regarded as "legal" or "contractual" rather than "sacramental" in character (and is legally terminable), Bengali Muslims speak of the relationship of husband and wife as a "shared body" relationship in which the wife is the "half-body" of her husband.[1] In other words, there is a level at which we may speak of "Bengali kinship" without regard to differences between Muslims and Hindus.

There is another level, however, at which a significant difference appears between Muslims and Hindus: this is the level of the clan (*kula*). For Hindus, the clan is unified by sharing the bodily substance of its common seed male (*bīja-puruṣa*). Muslims, by contrast, appear to draw a fundamental distinction between the living and the dead and to regard deceased ancestors as no longer part of the same order as living persons. Whereas Hindus feed and worship their ancestors, Muslims do not. When Hindus speak of *kula* they refer to the shared body relationship and the sharing code for conduct appropriate for *jñāti* whether they are living or dead. For Muslims, the sharing relationship of *jñāti* appears generally to be thought of as terminated by death. Thus, Muslims do not usually speak of their *kula*[2] but, most commonly, of their *vaṃśa* or *goṣṭhī*. As we noted earlier (chap. 1), the terms *vaṃśa* and *goṣṭhī* are derived from Sanskrit and are sometimes used by Hindus as synonyms for *kula*. However, *kula* is distinguished from these other terms by its emphasis on the sharing of the body of the common deceased ancestral male.

Terminology

There are no differences in the patterning of kinship terms used by Muslims and Hindus. Over the last several decades, however, there has been a tendency among Bengali Muslims, beginning in the cities and spreading to the rural areas, to replace words identified as "Hindu" with distinctively "Muslim" terms. In the kinship vocabularly terminological differences between the two groups consist of (*a*) seven terms for classes of kinsmen which, together with their modified forms, are distinctively Muslim synonyms for Hindu terms discussed in the text; and (*b*) distinctively Muslim honorific modifiers which replace the "paternal" modifiers used by Hindus.

The seven kinship terms used by Muslims in Bengali are borrowed from Urdu. Among them, two, *ābbā* ("father"), and *khālā* ("mother's sister"), are derived from Arabic; one, *phuphu* ("father's sister"), is from Persian. The remainder—*nānā* ("mother's father"), *āmmā* ("mother"), *cācā* ("father's brother"),[3] and *bhābi* ("elder brother's wife")—are derived from Sanskrit forms of the eight basic terms. Derivative terms are formed from the Muslim terms by changing their gender and compounding them in exactly the same ways we discussed earlier. For example, the husband of *phuphu* is termed *phuphā*, and the son of one's *khālā* is termed *khālāto-bhāi*.

Although Muslims distinguish among siblings of the same sex according to the order of their birth, they often use *bhāi* rather than *dādā* to designate elder brothers, reserving the latter term for father's father and those whom he calls "brother." Similarly, elder sister is not designated as *didi*, but there appear to be a number of dialectal synonyms such as *bubu* and *āpā* that may be used to designate persons of this class.

The paternal modifiers *ṭhākur*, *maśāy*, and *bābu* that are used by Hindus to elevate the dignity of kinship terms when they are applied to senior males are not used by Muslims. A distinctively Muslim set of modifiers is used in their place. These are *sāheb* (from Arabic), meaning "respectable" or "noble," *miyā* (from Persian), meaning "master" or "foremost," and *jān* (Persian), meaning "honored." Thus, father's father may be addressed as *dādā-miyā* or *dādā-sāheb*, father's elder brother as *jeṭhā-sāheb*, father's younger brother as *cācā-miyā* or *cācā-jān*, and wife's father as *śvaśura-sāheb*.

A Muslim married woman may refer to her husband's father as *śvaśura-sáheb* but address him as *ābbā-jān*. She may refer to her husband's elder brothers as *bhāśura* but address them as *baṛo-miyā*, *mejo-miyā*, and so forth, according to the order of their birth. In situations where Hindus identify senior females as "mothers" by compounding the term *mā* with another kinship term, Muslims do so by compounding the term with *āmmā*. Thus, for example, *nānī-āmmā* ("mother's mother"), means "mother who is a mother's mother," and *khālā-āmmā* ("mother's sister"), means "mother who is a mother's sister."

Although there are some lexical differences between the kinship terms and the "nonkinship" modifiers used by Hindus and Muslims in Bengal, the patterns exhibited in the terminology are the same for the two groups.[4] Thus, it would seem reasonable to regard distinctively Hindu and Muslim terms as variants of a single Bengali pattern. The set of distinctively Muslim terms is given in table 8.

Periods of Death and Birth Impurity

Appendix 3

A precise illustration of the Hindu system for classifying kinsmen can be seen in the varying periods of "impurity" (*aśauca*) which a person has traditionally been seen to undergo upon the death or birth of a *jñāti* or *kuṭumba*. The whole question of impurity among Hindus is a complex one which, in our view, needs to be thoroughly reexamined in the light of the Hindu cultural categories we are attempting to elucidate. The material, which we present all too briefly here, is derived largely from contemporary written sources—the astrological almanacs (*pañjikā*) and the manuals (*paddhati*) used by domestic priests in Bengal. These of course are applications of the rules set down in the Sanskrit *śāstra*s or code books. The major source we have used here is the *Aśauca Vyavasthā* ("Arrangements for Impurity") section of a recent almanac (*Pañjikā* 1974/75, pp. 37–40 of the front matter), which is the authority most commonly consulted by Bengalis. But see also *Aśauca-vyavasthā* (1872, p. 1) and *Śabdakalpadrumaḥ* (s.v. *aśauca*). Virtually all the Bengali authorities base themselves on the great sixteenth-century Bengali expert on the *śāstra*s, Raghunandana Bhaṭṭācārya (1907). For a summary of the rules on impurity in other, earlier sources see Kane (1930–62, 4:267–307).

The birth or death of one of "one's own people" has been thought of in Bengal as potentially dangerous for both the newborn child or dead person and all those who share his body. This threat to their bodily well-being (*śārīrika-maṅgala*) comes not from "physical" contact with "polluting" bodily substances, such as blood, afterbirth, or corpses, but from the separation of the bodies involved and the radical transformations of bodily relationships which both birth and death are seen to entail. Thus, the periods of impurity are said to start with the separating act which begins the transformation, not from the time of either the birth or the death or of contact with "impure" substances. For birth, the separating act is the cutting of the umbilical cord, for death, the firing of the body on the funeral bier.

From these moments of separation onward, contact or contagion does enter the picture; persons who have bodily connections with the newly born or deceased become impure. During this period, the affected person lacks the competence (*adhikāra*) to engage in his usual acts of worship; that is, he is unable to come into contact with the gods, and his body is considered untouchable (*aspṛśya*) to others not so affected. One might say that the affected person himself enters a state approximating death, symbolized by abstinence from certain life-renewing activities such as eating normal food, shaving, changing into fresh clothes, bathing, and the like. The period of impurity ends with the resumption of these activities, all of which may be taken to symbolize his "rebirth" as a normal person.

The major distinction which concerns us here, from the point of view of the Hindu system of kin classification, is the distinction between a "full" (*pūrṇa*) or "heavy" (*guru*) period (*kāla*) of impurity (*aśauca*) and a "partial" (*khaṇḍa*) or "light" (*laghu*) period of impurity. The period of full impurity varies by *varṇa* (caste), being shorter for the higher and longer for the lower *varṇa*s, as shown in table 9. Periods of partial impurity do not for the most part vary by caste but do vary in length. These are one day (including the night), two days (including the intervening night),[1] and three days (including the two intervening nights).

The period of impurity also varies in length with the age of the dead person and/or the number of *saṃskāra*s, "preparatory" or life-cycle rites, he or she has undergone. Generally speaking, the period of death impurity is reduced for young, uninitiated, and unmarried persons. The point at which a person who dies is considered capable of causing the full period of impurity for relatives varies by *varṇa* (caste) and sex. A Brahman male who is past the age of six years and three months or who has been "prepared" (*saṃskṛta*) by the initiation (*upanayana*) ceremony may cause the full period of *aśauca* for certain relatives.[2] Śūdra males, not competent to undergo the Vedic initiation ceremony, are declared capable of causing full impurity after the age of six years or after marriage, this being the *saṃskāra* that makes a Śūdra into an adult.[3] For women of all castes, marriage is the decisive act which makes her "prepared." After this, her death may cause certain of her relatives to incur the full period of impurity.[4] In the discussion of death and birth impurity that follows, the reference is to a mature or adult person, one who has "come of age" (*vayaska*) or been properly prepared (*saṃskṛta*, see chap. 3).

The sharing of a place or living together is seen to generate a kinship relationship in Bengali culture. Hence, it is no surprise to find that residence also affects the length of the period of impurity. The sharing of a place of residence, even on a temporary basis, may increase a period of partial impurity by one day, but only to a maximum of three days.

The data on periods of death impurity for men and women are given in tables 10 and 11. The specific *sapiṇḍa*s listed in both tables are placed in parentheses because they are not listed individually in the sources. Since the relationships included in the *sapiṇḍa* class for the purpose of death impurity are many more than those listed, these lists are not exhaustive. The lists of *asapiṇḍa*s are, however, exhaustive. If one compares these lists with tables 2 through 7 one can see that many residual *jñāti* and *kuṭumba* for which there are specific terms are not listed. This means simply that no period of *aśauca* is compulsory when these persons die.

Even a cursory glance at the tables shows that the contrast between *sapiṇḍa* and *asapiṇḍa* relationships is crucial in explaining variations in periods of impurity for both men and women. As we have seen, the term *sapiṇḍa*, meaning "of the same body," is sometimes used to refer to both par excellence and residual *jñāti*, to persons related by the same "seed" (semen) and to those related by "uterus" (*yoni*). Here, however, the term is clearly used to designate the largest set of par excellence *jñāti* alone, the set of men—and their wives—who share the body of their seventh ascending ancestral father.[5] In other words, a man incurs a full period of impurity when any of his par excellence *jñāti* dies. It seems then that the relatively close sharing of "seed" or semen entails the fullest transmission of impurity to all those who share it.

Virtually all of the persons for whom a man or woman incurs a partial period of death impurity are those classed by the texts as *asapiṇḍa*s, those not sharing the body of the same seventh ancestral male. As one can see, persons of the same clan who share the body of more remote ancestral males—*sakulya*s (who share the body of an eighth to tenth ancestral male) and *samānodaka*s (who share the body of an eleventh to fourteenth ancestral male) are classed here with the residual *jñāti* of other clans such as those of his mother's clan (e.g., mother's father, mother, and brother). Here we can see that the uterus is considered less capable of transmitting the potential for impurity than is semen, for relatives remotely related by semen are seen to incur the same period of impurity as relatives more closely related by uterine substance.

So far as the variations in the partial periods are concerned, it is clear that the period of impurity is less for the three *kuṭumba*s listed—wife's father, mother, and brother—than for the residual *jñāti*, for the former do not share a body with a man, while the latter do. On the other hand, some of the variations call for special explanations, as do some of the relationships which are included in and excluded from the lists by the sources. Since, however, all the Bengali listings fall within the rather wide range of variation exhibited in the *śāstra*s with respect to *asapiṇḍa*s, the Bengali choices seem to be matters of stress rather than of "fundamental" kin classification.[6] The only listings that need further explication here are those of sister and daughter.

Sisters and daughters who are classed as *sapiṇḍa*s of their brothers and parents before marriage appear only as *asapiṇḍa*s in the tables. This is to be explained by the effect marriage has on a woman's relationships. The tables show only the periods of impurity caused by mature or prepared persons. A woman is considered unprepared before marriage. Once married, she becomes a *sapiṇḍa* of her husband and his *sapiṇḍa*s and ceases to be a *sapiṇḍa* of her father and brother. Consequently, the death of a sister or daughter never causes full impurity for her brother or parents. Before her marriage she causes only a reduced period because she is immature or unprepared, while after her marriage, transformed into a *sapiṇḍa* of her husband, she causes full impurity only for him and his *sapiṇḍa*s.

The rule enjoining no period of impurity for a mother or father on the death of their married daughter, a departure from the general rule enjoining a period of two days for close *asapiṇḍa*s, is not universal in the *śāstra*s and, again, seems to be a matter more of stress than of kin classification,[7] underlining the fact that once married, the daughter is a *sapiṇḍa* of her husband and no longer of her parents.

The position of the *dattaka-putra*, the son who is "given" or, as we would say, "adopted," is of some interest. If such a son is already a *sapiṇḍa*, then his death causes a full period of impurity to be incurred and, conversely, the death of one of his *sapiṇḍa*s causes a period of full impurity for him. On the other hand, if he is an *asapiṇḍa*, then the period of impurity is a partial one—three days, as in the case of the mother's father. The adopted son's wife, son, and all persons who share his body in the more ordinary way incur full periods of impurity when any of them dies. This treatment of the adopted son illustrates the contrast between the bodies of males and females. The body of a male is "hard"; hence, when a son who is an *asapiṇḍa* is "given" he cannot be transformed into a *sapiṇḍa*. The body of a female is, however, "soft"; hence, when a daughter is "given," she is transformed into a *sapiṇḍa*. This contrast helps to explain why a man who does not have a son of his own body, but has a daughter, generally prefers not to adopt a son and instead gives his daughter and her son his wealth at the time of his death.

Finally, it should be noted that the category *asapiṇḍa*, meaning "not of the same (ancestral male) body" and used in the texts to denote persons for whom a man or woman incurs death impurity, is an open one. Some persons who are not related by shared or given body and are not considered to be either *jñāti* or *kuṭumba* are also included among the *asapiṇḍa*s for whom a person incurs a partial period of death impurity. Such, for example, are the *guru*, the *guru*'s wife, the fellow student (*sahādhyāyī*), and the king (*maṇḍalādhipati*). These are persons to whom one is related not by bodily substance but by other substances that symbolize well-being and solidarity, as discussed on pages 32–34. Even though they are not classed as *jñāti* or *kuṭumba*, they are considered to fall within the larger class of *ātmīya-svajana*, "one's own people."

The impurity caused by birth (*jananāśauca*) is, except for the genetrix or mother, neither as severe nor—with respect to the relatives affected—as extensive as the impurity caused by death. Only the *sapiṇḍa* relatives of a newborn, living male or female incur the full period of impurity; the *asapiṇḍa* relatives by and large do not.[8] Furthermore, the period of untouchability caused by birth is ended immediately for all *sapiṇḍa*s but the mother by bathing. For the mother, however, the period of untouchability lasts ten days if she is of a twice-born caste, thirteen days if a Śūdra. The total period of impurity for the mother is also longer. For a twice-born woman, it is twenty days if she gives birth to a son, thirty if she gives birth to a daughter. For a Śūdra woman, it is thirty days in both cases. This entire period is known as the *sūtikāśauca*, the period of "parturition impurity." Throughout this period the mother is to be kept in a special parturition hut (*sūtikā-gṛha*) constructed for the purpose of delivering the child and confining the impurity caused by it.

Tables

Appendix 4

TABLE 1 The Eight Basic Kinship Terms and Their Synonyms

G^{+1}	*bābā/pitā, tāta; mā/mātā*	Fa; Mo
G^{0}	*svāmī, pati; strī, patnī, bou/vadhū, jāyā*	Hu; Wi
	bhāi/bhrātā	Br
	bon/bhaginī	Si
G^{-1}	*chele, po/putra*	So
	meye, jhi/duhitā, kanyā	Da

NOTE: In this and subsequent tables, terms are organized by generations ascending (+) and descending (−) from ego's own generation (G^{0}). Bengali terms are given first, and where the Sanskrit equivalent is different it is given second, separated by a diagonal (/). Alternative terms are separated by a comma; terms for wives of males first given on a line are separated by a semicolon.

TABLE 2 Terms for a Man's Par Excellence *Jñāti*

G^{+3}	*po-bābā/prapitāmaha; jhi-mā/prapitāmahī*	FaFaFa; FaFaMo
G^{+2}	*ṭhākur-dādā/pitāmaha; ṭhākur-mā/pitāmahī*	FaFa; FaMo
G^{+1}	*bābā/pitā, tāta; mā/mātā*	Fa; Mo
	pitṛvya; pitṛvya-patnī	FaBr; FaBrWi
	jeṭhā/jyeṣṭha-tāta; jeṭhī	FaElBr; FaElBrWi
	khuṛā, kākā/khulla-tāta; khuṛī, kākī	FaYoBr; FaYoBrWi
	(pisī/pitṛ-ṣvasā)	FaSi
G^{0}	*bhāi/bhrātā; bhrātṛ-jāyā*	Br; BrWi
	dādā; bhāj, bou-di	ElBr; ElBrWi
	bou-mā/bhrátṛ-vadhū	YoBrWi

TABLE 2 continued

	(bon/bhaginī)	Si
	(didi)	ElSi
	pitṛvya-putra	FaBrSo
	jeṭhtuto- bhāi; bou-di; bou-mā	FaElBrSo; FaElBrSoWi(El); FaElBrSoWi(Yo)
	khuṛtuto- bhāi; bou-di; bou-mā	FaYoBrSo; FaYoBrSoWi(El); FaYoBrSoWi(Yo)
	(pitṛvya-kanyā)	FaBrDa
	(jeṭhtuto-bon)	FaElBrDa
	(khuṛtuto-bon)	FaYoBrDa
	bou/vadhū, strī, patnī, jāyā	Wi
G^{-1}	*chele, po/putra; bou-mā/putra-vadhū*	So; SoWi
	(meye, jhi/duhitā, kanyā)	Da
	bhāi-po/bhrātṛvya, bhrātuṣputra; bhāi-po-bou	BrSo; BrSoWi
	(bhāi-jhi/bhrātuṣkanyā)	BrDa
G^{-2}	*nāti/pautra; nāt-bou*	SoSo; SoSoWi
	(nātnī/pautrī)	SoDa

NOTE: Terms for females who are classed as par excellence *jñāti* before marriage but as residual *jñāti* or *kuṭumba* after marriage are enclosed in parentheses.

TABLE 3 Terms for a Man's Residual *Jñāti* or *Kuṭumba*

G^{+2}	*dādā-maśāy/mātāmaha;* *didi-mā/mātāmahī*	MoFa; MoMo
G^{+1}	*māmā/mātula; māmī/mātulānī*	MoBr; MoBrWi
	māsī/mātṛ-ṣvasā	MoSi
G^{0}	*ātma-bandhu*	
	pistuto-bhāi	FaSiSo
	māmāto-bhāi	MoBrSo
	māstuto-bhāi	MoSiSo
	pistuto-bon	FaSiDa
	māmāto-bon	MoBrDa
	māstuto-bon	MoSiDa

TABLE 3 continued

G^{-1}	*bhāgne/bhāgineya; bhāgnā-bou*	SiSo; SiSoWi
	bhāgnī/bhāgineyī	SiDa
G^{-2}	*nāti/dauhitra*	DaSo
	nātnī/dauhitrī	DaDa

NOTE: The classes of female kin indicated within parentheses in table 2 are also classed as residual *jñāti* or *kuṭumba* after they are married.

TABLE 4 Terms for a Man's *Kuṭumba*

G^{+2}	*dādā-śvaśura; didi-śāśuṛī*	WiFaFa; WiFaMo
G^{+1}	*śvaśura; śāśuṛī/śvaśrū*	Wi Fa; WiMo
	jāṭ-śvaśura; jāṭ-śāśuṛī	WiFaElBr; WiFaElBrWi
	khuṛ-śvaśura; khuṛ-śāśuṛī	WiFaYoBr; WiFaYoBrWi
	pis-śvaśura; pis-śāśuṛī	WiFaSiHu; WiFaSi
	māmā-śvaśura; māmī-śāśuṛī	WiMoBr; WiMoBrWi
	mās-śvaśura; mās-śāśuṛī	WiMoSiHu; WiMoSi
	tāoi; māoi	Br or SiSpFa; Br or SiSpMo
	pise	FaSiHu
	meso	MoSiHu
G^{0}	*śālā/śyālā; śālāj*	WiBr; WiBrWi
	śālī/śyālī; bhāyrā-bhāi	WiSi; WiSiHu
	beyāi/vaivāhika; beyān/vaivāhikī	So or DaSpFa; So or DaSpMo
	bhaginī-pati	SiHu
G^{-1}	*śālā-po*	WiBrSo
	śālā-jhi	WiBrDa
	śālī-po	WiSiSo
	śālī-jhi	WiSiDa
	jāmāi/jāmātā	DaHu
	bhāi-jhi-jāmāi	BrDaHu
	bhāgnī-jāmāi	SiDaHu
G^{-2}	*nāt-jāmāi*	SoDaHu

TABLE 5 Terms for a Married Woman's Par Excellence *Jñāti*

G^{+2}	*dādā-śvaśura; didi-śāśuṛī*	HuFaFa; HuFaMo
G^{+1}	*śvaśura, ṭhākur, ṭhākur-bāp*	HuFa
	śāśuṛī/śvaśrū, ṭhākruṇ, mā-ṭhākruṇ	HuMo
	jāṭ-śvaśura; jāṭ-śāśuṛī	HuFaElBr; HuFaElBrWi
	khuṛ-śvaśura; khuṛ-śāśuṛī	HuFaYoBr; HuFaYoBrWi
G^{0}	*svāmī, pati*	Hu
	devara; jā/yātṛ	HuBr; HuBrWi
	bhāśura, baṛo-ṭhākur/bhrātṛ-śvaśura	HuElBr
	deor, ṭhākur-po	HuYoBr
G^{-1}	*chele; bou-mā*	So; SoWi
	(meye)	Da
	bhāśura-po	HuElBrSo
	(bhāśura-jhi)	HuElBrDa
	deor-po	HuYoBrSo
	(deor-jhi)	HuYoBrDa
G^{-2}	*nāti/pautra; nāt-bou*	SoSo; SoSoWi
	(nātnī)	SoDa

TABLE 6 Terms for a Married Woman's Residual *Jñāti* or *Kuṭumba*

G^{+3}	*po-bābā; jhi-mā*	FaFaFa; FaFaMo
G^{+2}	*ṭhākur-dādā; ṭhākur-mā*	FaFa; FaMo
	dādā-maśāy; didi-mā	MoFa; MoMo
G^{+1}	*bābā; mā*	Fa; Mo
	jeṭhā; jeṭhī	FaElBr; FaElBrWi
	khuṛā; khuṛī	FaYoBr; FaYoBrWi
	pisī	FaSi
	māmā; māmī	MoBr; MoBrWi
	māsī	MoSi
	pis-śāśuṛī	HuFaSi
	māmā-śvaśura; māmī-śāśuṛī	HuMoBr; HuMoBrWi
	mās-śāśuṛī	HuMoSi

TABLE 6 continued

G^0	*bhāi; bhāj*	Br; BrWi
	bon	Si
	nanod, ṭhākur-jhi/nanandā	HuSi
	jeṭhtuto-bhāi	FaElBrSo
	jeṭhtuto-bon	FaElBrDa
	khuṛtuto-bhāi	FaYoBrSo
	khuṛtuto-bon	FaYoBrDa
	pistuto-bhāi	FaSiSo
	pistuto-bon	FaSiDa
	māmāto-bhāi	MoBrSo
	māmāto-bon	MoBrDa
	māstuto-bhāi	MoSiSo
	māstuto-bon	MoSiDa
G^{-1}	*bhāi-po; bhāi-po-bou*	BrSo; BrSoWi
	bhāi-jhi	BrDa
	bon-po	SiSo
	bon-jhi	SiDa
	bhāgne; bhāgnā-bou	HuSiSo; HuSiSoWi
	bhāgnī	HuSiDa
G^{-2}	*nāti/dauhitra*	DaSo
	nātnī/dauhitrī	DaDa

TABLE 7 Terms for a Married Woman's *Kuṭumba*

G^{+1}	*pise*	FaSiHu
	meso	MoSiHu
	pis-śvaśura	HuFaSiHu
	mās-śvaśura	HuMoSiHu
G^0	*bhaginī-pati*	SiHu
	nandāi, ṭhākur-jāmāi	HuSiHu
G^{-1}	*jāmāi*	DaHu
G^{-2}	*nāt-jāmāi*	SoDaHu

NOTE: In descending generations a married woman's *jāmāi*s are the same as her husband's.

TABLE 8 Distinctively Muslim Kinship Terms

G^{+2}	*nānā; nānī*	MoFa; MoMo
G^{+1}	*ābbā; āmmā*	Fa; Mo
	cācā; cācī	FaBr; FaBrWi
	phuphu; phuphā	FaSi; FaSiHu
	khālā; khālu	MoSi; MoSiHu
G^{0}	*cācāto-bhāi*	FaBrSo
	cācāto-bon	FaBrDa
	phuphāto-bhāi	FaSiSo
	phuphāto-bon	FaSiDa
	khālāto-bhāi	MoSiSo
	khālāto-bon	MoSiDa
	bhābi	ElBrWi

NOTE: Classes of kinsmen designated by terms in this list are categorized as *jñāti*, residual *jñāti* or *kuṭumba*, or *kuṭumba* as shown in tables 2 through 7.

TABLE 9 Periods of Full Impurity by Caste

Brāhmaṇa	10 days
Kṣatriya	12 days
Vaiśya	15 days
Śūdra	30 days

TABLE 10 Periods of Death Impurity Incurred by a Man

Relationship	Period: Full 10–30d[1]	Partial 3d, 2n	Partial 2d, 1n	Partial 1d, 1n	None
Sapiṇḍa	(FaFa				
	FaMo				
	FaBr				
	FaBrWi				
	Fa				
	Mo				
	Wi				
	Br				
	BrWi				
	FaBrSo				
	FaBrSoWi				
	So				
	SoWi				
	SoSo				
	SoSoWi				
	etc.)				
Asapiṇḍa		MoFa	MoMo	MoFaSiSo[4]	Da
		and	FaSi	MoMoBrSo[4]	
		sakulya	MoBr	MoMoSiSo[4]	
			MoBrWi	WiFa	
			MoSi	WiMo	
			FaFaSiSo[2]	WiBr	
			FaMoBrSo[2]		
			FaMoSiSo[2]		
			Si		
			FaSiSo[3]		
			MoBrSo[3]		
			MoSiSo[3]		
			SiSo		
			DaSo		
			and		
			samānodaka		

[1]d=day, n=night.
[2]Classed as *pitṛ-bandhu*, see pp. 117–18, n. 4.
[3]Classed as *ātma-bandhu*, see pp. 117–18, n. 4.
[4]Classed as *mātṛ-bandhu*, see pp. 117–18, n. 4.

TABLE 11 Periods of Death Impurity Incurred by a Married Woman

Relationship	Period				
	Full	Partial			None
	10–30d	3d, 2n	2d, 1n	1d, 1n	
Sapiṇḍa	(HuFaFa				
	HuFaMo				
	HuFaBr				
	HuFaBrWi				
	HuFa				
	HuMo				
	Hu				
	HuBr				
	HuBrWi				
	HuFaBrSo				
	HuFaBrSoWi				
	So				
	SoWi				
	SoSo				
	SoSoWi				
	etc.)				
Asapiṇḍa		Fa			
		Mo			

Notes

CHAPTER 1

[1]This usage in Bengali dates at least to the sixteenth century (see Mukundarāma 1962, p. 180). Another term, *bandhu*, meaning "one who is tied," was used in conjunction with the term *jñāti*; in the sixteenth century it was used perhaps even more frequently than its synonym *kuṭumba* (see Mukundarāma 1962, pp. 128, 165). *Bandhu* could in certain contexts also be used as a synonym of *jñāti*, *jñāti-kuṭumba*, or even *ātmīya-svajana* (see Mukundarāma 1962, pp. 77, 176, 179). In modern usage, and especially in urban areas, *bandhu* has come to mean "friend," as opposed to *jñāti* or *kuṭumba*. The equivalent term in the Sanskrit *śāstra*s or code books is *jñāti-sambandhī* as, for example, in Manu 2.132, or, less frequently, *jñāti-bāndhava*, Manu 9.269. (Compiled by a school of specialists in North India between the second century B.C. and the second century A.D., the *Dharmaśāstra* of Manu has probably been the most influential of Hindu code books.) The term *bāndhava*, along with its alternate form *bandhu*, may be used in the Sanskrit *śāstra*s as it is in the Bengali texts, although it is generally not used to mean "friend" in the *śāstra*s and is given a kinship meaning not found in Bengali (see chap. 1, note 4).

[2]The families of others of one's own people may similarly be referred to by their houses, thus: *bāper bāṛi*, "father's house"; *śvaśura-bāṛi*, "spouse's father's house"; *boner bāṛi*, "sister's house"; *māmār bāṛi*, "mother's brother's house," or *jāmāi bāṛi*, "daughter's husband's house."

[3]The term *jñāti* denotes the same set of persons in its restricted usage in the Sanskrit *śāstra*s as well. For example, Kullūka Bhaṭṭa (thirteenth century) at Manu 2.132 states that it consists of "those on the father's side (*pitṛ-pakṣa*) beginning with the father's brothers (*pitṛvya*)" (Yogi 1966). Medhātithi (ninth century) at Manu 4.79 gives virtually the same definition (Jha 1932–39). See also the "Indigenous Account of Kinship" in Appendix 1.

[4]The existence of this set as a distinct category is confirmed in the *śāstra*s, where the term *bāndhava* (or *bandhu*) is often used to denote it. Manu 4.179 employs the triple compound *jñāti-sambandhī-bāndhava*. In

it, the word *bāndhava* is glossed by Medhātithi as "those of the mother's side (*mātṛ-pakṣa*) beginning with the mother's sister's son." At Manu 5.80 he states that this is a category beginning with the mother's brother (*mātula*) (Jha 1932–39). In connection with inheritance, three particular sets of *bandhu* are widely enumerated: *ātma-bandhu*, "one's own residual *jñāti*"—father's sister's son, mother's brother's son, and mother's sister's son; *pitṛ-bandhu*, "father's residual *jñāti*"—father's father's sister's son, father's mother's brother's son, and father's mother's sister's son; and *mātṛ-bandhu*—mother's father's sister's son, mother's mother's brother's son, and mother's mother's sister's son. Note that while all of these are related by shared bodily substance, none belongs to one's own, one's father's or one's mother's father's *kula*. A man and his father's brother's sons are said to share the same semen or "seed." The bodily substance shared by a man with his *bandhu*s listed above is, by contrast, uterine blood or womb. Hence these are sometimes considered to be *yoni-sambaddha*, "related by the uterus" (Vijñāneśvara on Yājñavalkya 3.24, in Shastri Pansikar 1918).

[5]See Vijñāneśvara at Yājñavalkya 1.52 (in Shastri Pansikar 1918). It may be surprising to find this definition of *sapiṇḍa* used in an account of Bengali kinship, since it is well known that in questions of inheritance the Mitākṣarā applies not to Bengal but to North India and elsewhere. The text used in Bengal, the twelfth-century *Dāyabhāga* of Jimutavāhana, stresses not the body but another symbolic feature in defining the *sapiṇḍa* relationship. A *piṇḍa* may be defined as a body; it may also be defined as the ball of food which constitutes a food offering (*piṇḍa-dāna* or *nirvāpa*) made to an ancestral father (*pitṛ*). Thus, another meaning of the term *sapiṇḍa* in the *śāstra*s is those who have the capacity to share in the same food offerings (either as givers or receivers). In other words, two shared substance features may be used to define the class of *sapiṇḍa*s, the one, human bodily substance, the other, food. (As we shall presently see, food is widely used to define and symbolize solidary relationships in Hindu culture.) The Mitākṣarā and Dāyabhāga use both of these features to characterize the *sapiṇḍa* relationship.

Jimutavāhana and Raghunandana, a sixteenth-century follower, nowhere deny that a class of persons sharing the same bodily substance exists (Raghunandana includes extracts from the Mitākṣarā definition of *sapiṇḍa*); and Vijñāneśvara does not discard the offering of food to *sapiṇḍa*s. Rather, each places different stress on these features; Vijñāneśvara holding that shared bodily substance is definitive while Jimutavāhana holds that the capacity to give and receive offerings of food is decisive. Some interesting consequences flow from this difference. Under Mitākṣarā, for example, a man's sons have a right to shares of his wealth before his death because they share bodily substance with him. Under Dāyabhāga, this right does not arise until after the father dies and receives his first offering of food from his eldest son because they are not, for purposes of inheritance, related by a *piṇḍa* offering until then. See Raghunandana's *Śuddhitattva* (1907, pp. 494–95, 498–99). For further discussion of this and other contrasts, see P. V. Kane (1930–62, 2:452–58, 472–77).

[6]The use of the term *jñāti* to denote sharing relatives beyond the closest eight also occurs in the *śāstra*s (see Manu 4.179–80), where a distinction is made between a man and his mother (*mātā*), father (*pitā*), sister (*jāmi*), brother (*bhrātā*), wife (*bhāryā*), and daughter (*duhitā*), on the one hand, and *jñāti, sambandhī*, and *bāndhava*, on the other. The "Indigenous Account" in Appendix 1 uses the terms *jñāti* and *bāndhava* to refer to even more distant sets of kin, namely, those for whom there are no specific kin terms.

[7]*Kuṭumba* has an additional meaning in Sanskrit (and also therefore in Bengali)—it may be used as a synonym for *jñāti*. In many parts of India this latter sense has taken precedence and *kuṭumba* or a word derived from it is used to designate the *goṣṭhī* (see, e.g., Mayer 1960, pp. 170–71; Madan 1965, pp. 181–82; Chauhan 1967, pp. 36–37). In Bengali, however, the most usual sense of *kuṭumba* excludes the par excellence *jñāti* set, and we have so used it here.

[8]This is the term used in the *śāstra*s to denote this class of people. Kullūka at Manu 2.132 states that it contains "those of the mother's side and those beginning with the wife's father," thereby including the set of residual *jñāti* within it (Yogi 1966). The term *bandhu* is sometimes used in the *śāstra*s in this sense as well. See Manu 2.207, where Medhātithi glosses the term as "one who is related to the clan (*vaṃśa-sambandhita*); and Manu 5.80, where he defines *bāndhavas* (plural) as "those beginning with the wife's brother (*śyālaka*) and the mother's sister's son (*mātṛ-ṣvasreya*)" (in Jha 1932–39). Occasionally the term *sambandhī* means simply "relative" (see Appendix 1). It appears in modern Bengali in a very restricted usage to designate the wife's elder brother.

[9]There is a great deal of discussion in social scientific literature about the actual incidence of "joint families" in Bengal and elsewhere in South Asia. Although such statistical rates have little bearing upon the cultural categories we discuss here, it is important to recognize that Bengali Hindus do not often violate their stated norms. Depending upon how "joint family" is defined, the data available indicate that from 35 to 55 percent of Bengali Hindu families are joint (Nicholas 1961; Basu 1962; Sarma 1964; Sen 1965; see Kolenda 1968 for definitions, comparisons, and a summary). However, in detailed house-to-house censuses of eleven West Bengal villages we asked the additional question of how many married men have separated their families (i.e., the sharing of food) from the families of their living fathers. The number is miniscule and the explanations—highly particular and unusual in each case—most often relate to some gross violation,

such as when a father "keeps a concubine" (*rāṛh-rākhā*) or a son "arranges his own marriage" (*nijer biyā karā*). In other words, it is our experience that almost all Bengalis live in families which, given the open-ended character of the family, have the potential for becoming "joint" in the course of time. Clearly, there are many instances in which, for a time, it is not possible for a family to be joint, namely, cases where an unmarried or newly married son's father is dead. Virtually all the "nuclear families" found in our censuses were of this kind. The vast literature on the joint family in India includes little detailed discussion of the issue of "eligibility" for family jointness, but see Orenstein and Micklin (1966) and Shah (1974, pp. 76–79).

[10]A list of gifts expected to be sent by an upper-caste man of moderate means to his daughter's husband's house on this occasion, in the month of Jyaiṣṭha (May-June), includes mangos, jackfruit, other seasonal fruits, ornate cakes made of ground pulses, a wooden stool, betel leaf, and towels. In addition, the daughter's husband should take back with him from his visit sweetened yogurt, a variety of special sweets, areca nut and spices, pairs of dhotis and shawls, vests, shirts, handkerchiefs, socks, shoes, scents, soaps, towels, a mirror, a comb and brush, and some prepared betel leaves (Bose, ca. 1929, p. 71).

[11]On this occasion, which occurs in the month of Āśvina (September-October), the bride's father should give his daughter's husband the same gifts as on Jāmāi-ṣaṣṭhī. In addition, he should send a garment (dhoti or sari) and a shawl to each person in his daughter's husband's family, and his daughter's husband should send a garment to each person in his wife's father's family (Bose, ca. 1929, p. 72).

[12]This ceremony, which occurs in the month of Kārtik (October-November), is also popularly called *bhāi-phõṭā* because of the auspicious mark (*phõṭā*) that a married sister is to place on the forehead of her brother (*bhāi*) The gift-giving relationship that a married sister has with her brother after her marriage is peculiarly distinguished—she gives her brother presents, a dhoti and a shawl, betel leaf, spices, and sweets, as well as feeding him special cooked food (Bose, ca. 1929, p. 72). Although most gifts follow the daughter to her husband's house, here is an example of gifts moving in the opposite direction.

[13]The ambiguity of the *purohita–yajamāna* relationship, discussed at length by Heesterman (1964), is reflected in the terms these two use to address one another. The *purohita* appears as a kind of household servant, but as a Brahman, he is addressed by the *yajamāna* as "lord," and, if he is older, as *ṭhākur-mahāśaya* "lord of great dignity." The *yajamāna* appears as a kind of patron, but one before whom the *purohita* should not humble himself. Therefore the *purohita* may use a variety of verbal devices, includ-

ing "no-naming," to avoid inferiorizing either himself or the *yajamāna* by placing one or the other clearly in the position of father or son.

Chapter 2

[1]If their fathers are alive, they are usually the *kartā*s of the bride and groom. However, if a father's father is alive he may play this role. If none of these men is alive, then another male *jñāti* takes on the role.

[2]*Prajāpati* also means "butterfly" in Bengali. Advantage is taken of this polysemy in marriage symbolism; figures of butterflies may be used to ornament the marriage site, the crowns that are worn by the bride and groom, and so forth.

[3]Nowadays the *uttara-vivāha* may in fact be performed in the house where the previous day's ritual took place; but the *purohita* and items used should be provided by the groom's father.

[4]This aspect of marriage symbolism is based on the traditional assumption that the bride is premenstrual. The vermilion is traditionally applied with a rice-measuring basket, symbolizing her womb as a receptacle of his seed.

[5]It is widely believed that having sexual relations on this night will lead to the death of the husband as it did in the case of Lakhindar in the Bengali myth of the snake goddess Manasā (see Dimock 1963, pp. 250–56).

[6]It is thought that if this ceremony is done on an odd-numbered day a female child will be procreated.

[7]In some listings this ceremony is called the *ṛtu*, or "menstrual" *saṃskāra*.

[8]According to the Hindu code books only men born in the three higher *varṇa*s—Brāhmaṇ, Kṣatriya, and Vaiśya—were competent to become twice-born. Throughout much of its history, however, the Hindu community of Bengal was said to have no Kṣatriyas and Vaiśyas. Hence only men of the Brāhmaṇ castes underwent the *upanayana*.

[9]A survey of Sanskrit education in Rajshahi District in 1836 indicates that the average Brahman pupil began studies at nine or ten years of age and finished between the ages of twenty-five and thirty-two years (Adam 1941, table 3, pp. 561–78).

[10]These are rice of the rainy season (*vrīhi*), rice of the autumn season (*śāli*), barley (*yava*), lentil (*mudga*), wheat (*godhuma*), sesame (*tila*), and mustard (*sarṣapa*).

Chapter 3

[1]While this assumption dates back at least to Morgan (1871), it persists at present in the technically sophisticated literature of "componential analysis" or "formal semantic analysis," where the expression "system of kin classification" is used in preference to "kinship terminology" and where the aim is "to discover the structure of the system, i.e., the criteria or 'rules' of kin classification that distinguish among and at the same time relate to one another the several categories belonging to any particular system" (Scheffler and Lounsbury 1971, p. 50).

[2]Fortes (1969, p. 58) speaks for a good many anthropologists when he says, "We all agree that a kinship terminology is a customary apparatus for the management of certain kinds of social relations." Dumont (1953) went further when he wrote of "the Dravidian kinship terminology as an expression of marriage."

[3]For example, a midwife is called *dāi-mā*, "mother who gives birth" and a religious ascetic may be addressed and referred to as *bābā-ji*, "revered father." Are these to be considered part of Bengali "kinship terminology"? For a full discussion of this problem see Schneider (1970).

[4]Of these eight terms, all of which are current in standard colloquial Bengali, three, *mā, bhāi*, and *bon*, are clearly *tadbhava*s; their *tatsama* forms are *mātā, bhrātā*, and *bhaginī*. Two, *svāmī* and *strī*, are *tatsamas*. Three, *bābā, chele*, and *meye*, are *tadbhava*s that have no *tatsama* forms.

[5]These four pairs of terms are examples of the class of copulative or *dvandva* compounds.

[6]Among the many synonyms for *chele*, probably the most important is the *tatsama* term *putra*, "son," and its *tadbhava* forms *put* and *po*. The term *meye* has the *tatsama* synonym *duhitā*, "daughter," and its *tadbhava* form *jhi*. In addition, a daughter to be married is spoken of as *kanyā* or *kone*, meaning "a female who desires (*kāmanā*) a husband."

[7]Synonyms for *svāmī* and *strī* include terms that point to their unity and complementarity as persons who share the same body—for example, *pati* ("lord") and *patnī* ("lady"); *bhartā* ("supporter") and *bhāryā* ("she who is supported"). Other pairs of terms point to the complementarity of male and female roles in the family and house—for example, *kartā* ("master") and *kartrī* ("mistress"), *gṛhastha* ("householder") and *gṛhinī* or *ginnī* ("female householder"). In addition, *strī* has the synonyms *vadhū* or *bou* ("she who is carried over") and *jāyā* ("she who gives birth"). A husband other than one's own may also be referred to by the term *jāmātā* or *jāmāi* ("he who accepts a *jāyā*").

[8]The term *bhāi* has the *tatsama* form *bhrātā*. The term *bon* has the *tatsama* form *bhaginī* and the alternate *ṣvasā*.

[9]Further siblings of the same sex may be added to the list by prefixing other adjectives such as *na-* ("new"), *rāṅgā-* ("colored'), *natun-* ("new"),

phul- ("flower"), *kane-* ("young"). All these adjectives may be applied to same-sex sibling sets and to their spouses throughout. Sarma (1951, pp. 60–61) discusses this usage pattern.

[10]Many of these are formed by "dependent" (*tatpuruṣa*) compounding, in which there is a genitive relationship between the last element and the former. An example of this kind is *bhāi-po* "son" (*po*) of "brother" (*bhāi*). A number of paternal and maternal terms are combined with other kinship terms to form compounds that are labeled by the Sanskrit grammarians "descriptive" (*karma-dhāraya*), in which the first member qualifies the second adjectivally. Some of these terms are used to designate particular classes of kinsmen, and some are used as alternates for other forms. An example of a descriptive compound is *bou-di* ("elder sister who is a wife," that is, "elder brother's wife").

[11]An example of this is *māmī* ("mother's brother's wife") from *māmā* ("mother's brother").

[12]Several *tatsama* terms are generated either by adding affixes to or strengthening basic terms. The term *pitṛvya* ("paternal one," viz., "father's brother") is generated by adding the suffix *-vya* to a term for father, *pitṛ*. An example of a term formed by strengthening a basic term is *pautra* ("son's son") from *putra* ("son").

[13]For example, one of the words for "father" (*dādā*), derived from *tāta*, and its feminine form *didi* or *dādī*, which are used in some contexts to designate elder siblings, are used in other contexts both to refer to and to address one's parents' parents.

[14]The term *jñāti* may be applied to the persons of the maximal family excluding the persons of the minimal family.

[15]Additional ancestral fathers (*pitṛ*) on both one's father's and one's mother's sides may be distinguished in Sanskrit, for example, *vṛddha-prapitāmaha* (FaFaFaFa), *ati-vṛddha-prapitāmaha* (FaFaFaFaFa), and *pramātāmaha* (MoFaFa), and so forth.

[16]*Ṭhākur-dādā/-mā* are *tatpuruṣa* compounds. The word *ṭhākur* here is a synonym for "father," hence these terms mean "father's father" and "father's mother." *Dādā-maśāy* and *didi-mā*, by contrast, are *karma-dhāraya* compounds used here simply to differentiate the mother's parents from those of the father.

[17]This term is generated by adding the suffix *-la* to a term for mother, *mātṛ*.

[18]In Sanskrit, by contrast, the term for a father's brother's wife is a dependent compound, *pitṛvya-patnī*, "wife of a paternal one," while the term for a mother's brother's wife, *mātulānī*, is formed by a gender change.

[19]These are shortened forms of the *tatpuruṣa* compounds *pitṛ-ṣvasā* ("sister of father") and *mātṛ-ṣvasā* ("sister of mother").

[20]The relative ages of ego and the kinsman in question influence the application of the compound terms that signal this pattern.

[21]Like the terms *svāmī* and *ṭhākur, maśāy* and *bābu* are "nonkinship" words, even though the term *bābu* is derived from a kinship term, *bābā* ("father"). The term *maśāy* (*mahāśaya*) means literally "he whose dignity is great."

[22]These are *karma-dhāraya* or descriptive compounds: *māsī-mā* means "mother who is mother's sister," and *māmā-bābu*, "the paternal one who is mother's brother."

[23]First noted by Blunt (1912, pp. 233–36), this use of the term for "brother" has been more recently examined by Dumont (1962, pp. 27–29) and Vatuk (1969, pp. 101–2).

[24]The *tatsama* or Sanskrit terms for these are: *pitṛvya-putra/-kanyā, mātula-putra/-kanyā, pitṛ-ṣvaseya/-ā*, and *mātṛ-ṣvaseya/-ā*.

[25]The distinction between *jñāti* of the same generation and the same *kula* and *jñāti* of the same generation but other *kula*s appears in the technical Sanskrit texts on inheritance, where males of the latter set are classed together as *ātma-bandhu* (see chap. 1, note 4).

[26]A man rarely uses the term *bhāj*, and then only to refer to an elder brother's wife. Men normally use the compound terms *bou-di* or *bou-ṭhākruṇ* to designate an older brother's wife and *bou-mā* for a younger brother's wife.

[27]These are *tadbhava* forms of *bhrātuṣ-putra* and *bhrātuṣ-kanyā*. The Sanskrit term *bhrātṛvya* is also used by Bengalis to mean "brother's son." Trautmann (1974, pp. 100–101, n. 44) has shown that the translation of this term in Sanskrit texts as "father's brother's son" is mistaken. The Bengali usage supports his findings.

[28]This is a *tadbhava* form of *bhāgineya*, itself a strengthened form of *bhaginī* ("sister").

[29]The same modifiers that a man uses to distinguish among his brothers and sisters may also be applied to the compound terms for their children, for example, *jeṭhtuto-bhāi-po, khuṛtuto-bhāgne*.

[30]This is a strengthened form of the Sanskrit term *duhitā*, "daughter."

[31]This is a *tadbhava* form of one of the many Sanskrit words for "son," *naptṛ*.

[32]One synonym for *bhāśur* is *jeṭh*, meaning simply "eldest."

[33]One etymology of *devara* is *dvitīya vara*, meaning "second husband" or "groom." This appears to reflect the fact that in some of the ancient *śāstra*s or code books a husband's brother might be appointed to beget a son upon his brother's widow (Bühler 1969, pp. 57–65). Inasmuch as this practice is not approved by contemporary Bengalis, they prefer to derive the term from *deva*, "god."

[34]T. N. Madan (1965, p. 233) says that among the Pandits of Kashmir "the only terms for affines which are common for a male and a female ego are *hihur* for HuFa/WiFa and *hash* for HuMo/WiMo, and all those terms for the siblings and parents of ego's parents-in-law which are derived from

hihur and *hash*. This is not as might have been expected. . . . The relations between a man and his parents-in-law are not identical with those between a woman and her parents-in-law."

[35]This is the case of the *ghar-jāmāi* or "marital son," who lives in his wife's father's house as a son.

Appendix 2

[1]Although the "heavy" Islamic portion of the Muslim marriage ritual is very different from the Hindu ceremony, the "women's rites" are very similar.

[2]However, even here exceptions are found. Nizam Uddin Ahmed (1968, pp. 157–58), reporting on kinship groupings in five Muslim villages about twenty miles north of Dacca, notes the use of the term *kula*, stating that it is not as commonly used as *vaṃśa* but that he "could not find out the reasons for this."

[3]If the term *jeṭhā* is retained for father's elder brother, as it is among some Muslims, then *cācā* is used to refer to father's younger brother. See, for example, Hara (1967, Appendix A).

[4]Some differences of usage patterns arise from the fact that there are cousin marriages among Muslims but not among Hindus. A man who married his mother's brother's daughter reported that he continued to address his wife's father as *māmā* but began addressing her mother as *āmmā* after his marriage. Similarly, his wife continued to address his mother as *phuphu* but began addressing his father as *ābbā* or *ābbā-jān*.

Appendix 3

[1]This period is termed a *pakṣiṇī* in the *śāstra*s.

[2]The period of *aśauca* for the *sapiṇḍa*s of a Brahman boy who dies between the ages of ten days and six years, three months, and is uninitiated, ranges from one to three days.

[3]The period of impurity for the *sapiṇḍa*s of a Śūdra boy who dies between the ages of one month and six years and is unmarried ranges from three to twelve days.

[4]Before marriage a daughter who dies causes her *sapiṇḍa*s to undergo a period of *aśauca* of three days or less.

[5]The extent of the *sapiṇḍa* relationship for an unmarried daughter is less than for a son. Her *sapiṇḍa*s are persons who share the seed of her father's father's father. Persons sharing the body of more remote ancestral fathers (up to the tenth generation counting the daughter) are classed as her *sakulya*s.

[6]The extra day of impurity incurred on the death of the mother's father is probably due to the fact that his daughter's son may, under certain cir-

cumstances, perform his last rites and inherit his wealth. Conversely, the inclusion of such persons as FaFaSiSo and MoMoBrSo appears to be connected with their place as potential heirs. For more data on the variations in the *śāstra*s, see Kane (1930–62, 4:278–80).

[7]Some of the *śāstra*s do in fact prescribe a period of two days on the death of a married daughter. See Kane (1930–62, 4:278).

[8]A woman in Bengal often prefers to give birth to her first child in her father's house. If she does, then the sharing of the same residence causes her father and mother to incur a period of impurity lasting three days.

References

Adam, William
1941 *Reports on the state of education in Bengal (1835 and 1838).* Anathnath Basu, ed. Calcutta: University of Calcutta.

Aśauca-vyavasthā
1872 *Etad-deśiya śuddhitattvādi smṛti-sammata aśauca-vyavasthā.* Calcutta: Bengal Superior Press.

Basu, Tara Krishna
1962 *The Bengal peasant from time to time.* Calcutta: Asia Publishing House.

Bhaṭṭācārya, Surendramohana, ed.
1973/74 *Purohita-darpaṇa.* 37th ed. Revised by Yogendracandra Vyākaraṇatīrtha Vidyāratna. Calcutta: Satyanārāyaṇa Library.

Bhattacharyya, Manibrata
1972 Rituals in tradition and modernity: A socio-ethnographic study of funeral rituals among the Hindus and semi-Hindu tribes of the Kangsabati valley, West Bengal. D.Sc. thesis, Department of Anthropology, University of Calcutta.

Blunt, E. A. H.
1912 *Census of India, 1911.* Vol. 15. *United Provinces of Agra and Oudh.* Part 1. *Report.* Allahabad: Superintendent, Government Press.

Bose, B. C.
ca. 1929 *Hindu customs in Bengal.* Calcutta: Book Company.

Bühler, Georg, trans.
1969 *The laws of Manu.* New York: Dover Publications. (Orig. pub. 1886 as vol. 25 of The Sacred Books of the East.)

Caṭṭopādhyāya, Becārāma
1864 *Gṛha-karmma.* Calcutta: Presidency Press.

Chakraberty, Chandra
1923 *An interpretation of ancient Hindu medicine.* Calcutta: Ramchandra Chakraberty.

Chakravarti, Nirmal
1935 An ethnic analysis of the culture-traits in the marriage customs as found among the Rāḍhīya Brahmins of Mymensingh. *Journal of the Department of Letters, University of Calcutta* 26:85–164.

Chatterjee (Śāstri), Heramba
1967 *Studies in some aspects of Hindu saṁskāra*s *in ancient India in the light of* Saṁskāratattva *of Raghunandana.* (Includes Sanskrit text.) Calcutta: Sanskrit Pustak Bhandar.

Chatterji, Suniti Kumar
1926 *Origin and development of the Bengali language.* 2 vols. Calcutta: University of Calcutta.

Chattopadhyay, Gouranga
1964 *Ranjana, a village in West Bengal.* Calcutta: Bookland Private Limited.

Chauhan, Brij Raj
1967 *A Rajasthan village.* New Delhi: Associated Publishing House.

Dāsa, Jñānendramohana
1937 *Bāṅgālā bhāṣār abhidhāna.* 2d ed. 2 vols. Calcutta: Indian Publishing House.

Day, Lal Behari
1888 *Bengal peasant life.* New ed. London: Macmillan.

De, Sushil Kumar
1952/53 *Bāṃlā pravāda.* Calcutta: A. Mukharji.

1961 *Vaiṣṇava faith and movement in Bengal.* 2d ed. Calcutta: Firma K. L. Mukhopadhyay.

Dimock, Edward C., Jr.
1963 *The thief of love: Bengali tales of court and countryside.* Chicago: University of Chicago Press.

Dumont, Louis
1953 The Dravidian kinship terminology as an expression of marriage. *Man* 53 (54):34–39.

1962 Le vocabulaire de parenté dans l'Inde du nord. *L'Homme* 2:7–48.

1966 Marriage in India: The present state of the question. III. North India in relation to South India. *Contributions to Indian Sociology* 9:90–114.

Fortes, Meyer
1962 Ritual and office in tribal society. In *Essays on the ritual of social relations*, ed. Max Gluckman. Manchester: Manchester University Press.

1969 *Kinship and the social order.* Chicago: Aldine Publishing Co.

Ghosh, Rajendrakumar
1931 *Kāyastha-samāja-tattva.* Calcutta: Rajendrakumar Ghosh.

Ghurye, G. S.
1946 Some kinship usages in Indo-Aryan literature. *Journal of the Anthropological Society of Bombay*, n.s., 1:1–80.

1955 *Family and kin in Indo-European culture.* Bombay: Oxford University Press.

Hara, Tadahiko
1967 *Paribar* and kinship in a Moslem rural village in East Pakistan. Ph.D. thesis, Department of Anthropology, Australian National University, Canberra.

Hazra, R. C.
1940 *Studies in the Puranic records on Hindu rites and customs.* Dacca: University of Dacca.

Heesterman, J. C.
1964 Brahmin, ritual and renouncer. *Wiener Zeitschrift für die Kunde Süd- und Ost-Asiens* 8:1–31.

James, Edwin O.
1974 *Encyclopaedia Britannica.* 15th ed., s.v. Sacraments.

Jha, Ganganatha, ed.
1932–39 Manu-smṛti, *with the* Manubhāṣya *of Medhātithi.* Bibliotheca Indica, no. 256. Calcutta: Asiatic Society of Bengal.

Kane, Pandurang Vaman
1930–62 *History of Dharmaśāstra.* 5 vols. Poona: Bhandarkar Oriental Research Institute.

Karve, Irawati
1938–39 Kinship terminology and kinship usages in *Rigveda* and *Atharvaveda*. *Annals of the Bhandarkar Oriental Research Institute* 20:69–96, 109–144.

1943–44 Kinship terms and the family organisation as found in the Critical Edition of the *Mahabharata*. *Bulletin of the Deccan College Research Institute* 5:61–148.

1965 *Kinship organization in India.* 2d ed. Bombay: Asia Publishing House.

Kolenda, Pauline M.
1968 Region, caste, and family structure: A comparative study of the Indian "joint" family. In *Structure and change in Indian society*, ed. M. Singer and B. S. Cohn. Chicago: Aldine Publishing Co.

Leach, Edmund R.
1958 Magical hair. *Journal of the Royal Anthropological Institute* 88:147–64.

Leaf, Murray J.
1971 The Punjabi kinship terminology as a semantic system. *American Anthropologist* 73:545–54.

Madan, T. N.
1965 *Family and kinship: A study of the Pandits of rural Kashmir.* Bombay: Asia Publishing House.

Marriott, McKim, and Inden, Ronald B.
1974 *Encyclopaedia Britannica.* 15th ed., s.v. Caste systems.

Mathur, K. S.
1964 *Caste and ritual in a Malwa village.* Bombay: Asia Publishing House.

Mayer, Adrian C.
1960 *Caste and kinship in Central India: A village and its region.* London: Routledge and Kegan Paul.

Morgan, Lewis Henry
1871 *Systems of consanguinity and affinity of the human family.* Smithsonian Contributions of Knowledge, no. 17. Washington, D.C.: Smithsonian Institution.

Mukherjee, Bhabananda
1962 Rajbanshi kinship system. *Bulletin of the Anthropological Survey of India* 11:47–65.

Mukhopādhyāya, Bhūdeva
1962/63 *Pārivārika prabandha* (originally pub. 1882). In *Bhūdeva-racanāsambhāra*, 2d ed., ed. Pramathanātha Biśī. Calcutta: Mitra and Ghosh.

Mukundarāma Cakravartī
1962 *Kavikaṅkana-Caṇḍī.* Part 1. Edited by Śrīkumār Bandyopādhyāya and Viśvapati Caudhuri. Calcutta: University of Calcutta.

Nicholas, Ralph W.
1961 Economics of family types in two West Bengal villages. *Economic Weekly* 13:1057–60.

Nizam Uddin Ahmed
1968 The peasant family and social status in East Pakistan. Ph.D. thesis, University of Edinburgh.

Orenstein, Henry, and Micklin, Michael
1966 The Hindu joint family: The norms and the numbers. *Pacific Affairs* 39:314–25.

Pandey, Raj Bali
1949 *Hindu* saṁskāras: *A socio-religious study of the Hindu sacraments.* Banaras: Vikrama Publications.

Pañjikā
1974/75 Gupta Press Directory *Pañjikā*, 1381.

Purāṇas
1909 *Brahmavaivarta Purāṇa.* Bombay: Śrīveṅkateśvara Steam Press.

Raghunandana Bhaṭṭācārya
1907 Smṛtiśāstram śuddhitattvam, *with commentaries* (ṭīkā) *by Kāśīrāma Vācaspati and Rādhāmohana Gosvāmi Bhaṭṭācārya.* 3d ed., Edited by Caṇḍīcaraṇa Smṛtibhūṣaṇa. Calcutta: Caṇḍīcaraṇa Smṛtibhūṣaṇa.

Rāya, Kṛṣṇavallabha
1903/4 *Baṅgīya Kāyastha samāja.* Calcutta.

Risley, H. H.
1892 *The tribes and castes of Bengal.* 2 vols. Calcutta: Bengal Secretariat Press.

Śabdakalpadrumaḥ
1931–34 [Sanskrit encyclopaedia in Bengali characters] 7 vols. Compiled by Rādhākānta Deva. Calcutta: New Bengal Press.

Sarma, Jyotirmoyee
1951 Formal and informal relations in the Hindu joint household of Bengal. *Man in India* 31:51–71.

1964 The nuclearization of joint family households in West Bengal. *Man in India* 44:193–206.

Scheffler, Harold W., and Lounsbury, Floyd G.
1971 *A study in structural semantics: The Siriono kinship system.* Englewood Cliffs, N.J.: Prentice-Hall.

Schneider, David M.
1968 *American kinship: A cultural account.* Englewood Cliffs, N.J.: Prentice-Hall.

1970 *What should be included in a vocabulary of kinship terms?* Proceedings of the Eighth Congress of Anthropological and Ethnological Sciences, Tokyo.

Sen, Lalit Kumar
1965 Family in four Indian villages. *Man in India* 45:1–16.

Sengupta, Rākhaladāsa (Kavirāja)
1913/14 *Prasūti-tantra, vā sacitra āyurvvedīya dhātri-vidyā.* Calcutta: Bidhūbhūṣaṇa Datta.

Sen Gupta, Sankar
1970 *A study of women of Bengal.* Calcutta: Indian Publications.

Shah, A. M.
1974 *The household dimension of the family in India.* Berkeley: University of California Press.

Shastri Pansikar, Wasudev Laxman, ed.
1918 Yajñavalkya-smṛti, *with the commentary* Mitākṣarā *of Vijñāneshvara.* 2d ed. Bombay: Nirnaya-sagar Press.

Trautmann, Thomas R.
1974 Cross-cousin marriage in ancient North India? In *Kinship and history in South Asia*, ed. T. R. Trautmann. Michigan Papers on South and Southeast Asia, no. 7. Ann Arbor: University of Michigan Center for South and Southeast Asian Studies.

Turner, Victor W.
1967 *The forest of symbols: Aspects of Ndembu ritual.* Ithaca: Cornell University Press.

1969 Introduction. In *Forms of symbolic action*, ed. Robert F. Spencer. Proceedings of the 1969 Annual Spring Meeting of the American Ethnological Society. Seattle: University of Washington Press.

van Gennep, Arnold
1960 The rites of passage. Translated by M. B. Vizedom and G. L. Caffee. Chicago: University of Chicago Press.

Vatuk, Sylvia
1969 A structural analysis of the Hindi kinship terminology. *Contributions to Indian Sociology*, n.s., 3:94–115.

Vidyāratna, Kālīprasanna, ed.
ca. 1970 *Āryyānuṣṭhāna paddhati.* 4 vols. Many printings. Revised and corrected by Ratneśvara Tantrajyotiṣaśāstrī. Calcutta: Sulabha Calcutta Library.

Woodroffe, John (pseud. Arthur Avalon), trans.
1963 *The great liberation* (*Mahānirvāna Tantra*). 4th ed. Madras: Ganesh.

Yogi, Satya Bhushan, ed.
1966 *The Manu Smṛti (chapters 1, 2), with Manvarthamuktāvalī of Kullūka, etc.* Delhi: Motilal Banarsidass.

Index

Ābhyudayika. See *Śrāddha*s
Adhivāsa, 41, 51
Adopted son, 73, 105–6
Affines, xvi, 9, 14, 16, 68–69, 83–84, 89
Age: and kinship terms, 69, 71, 73; and love, 25–26
Agnates, xvi, 9, 74
Agni-sthāpana, 45
Ancestors, 4–5, 14–15, 42, 64, 99–100
Anna-prāśana. See First feeding, ceremony of
Antyeṣṭi. See Final rites
Arghya, 43, 60
Asagotra, 4, 40
Aśmākramaṇa, 46
Āśramas. See Life-stages
Aṣṭa-kalāi. See Eight beans, ceremony of
Āṭ-kauṛe. See Eight beans, ceremony of
Ātma-bandhu, 118
Ātmīya-svajana ("one's own people"), 3–4, 71, 96; defining features of, 32–34, 88–89
Āyuṣya-karma, 56

Bāndhava, 95–96, 117–18, 119
Bandhu, 33, 117
Bāṛi ("house"), 7
Bāsā ("nest"), 7
Bāsar-ghar, 44
Bāsi-vivāha, 44
Beginning of study, rite of, 59
Bhakti. See Love, filial
Bhaṭṭācārya, Surendramohana, 39
Bhinna-gotra, 4
Bhojana, 49
Bhrātṛ-dvitīyā, 19
Bhrātṛ-prema. See Love, fraternal
Birth: and impurity, 106; and kinship terms, 70; and love, 22–23, 25–26; and marriage, 48; and *saṃskāras*, 55, 65–66, 91; second, for a Brahman, 59–60; second, for a Śūdra, 59; second, for a woman, 48
Blood, 3, 20, 21–22; uterine, 22, 52–54
Body: dead, cremation of, 62–63; dead, and *kula*, 5–8, 17; as defining feature, 13–14, 16–17, 87, 118; departed, 62–64; generation of, 52–54; gross, 63; living, and *parivāra*, 5–8, 17–18, 64; and love, 21–22, 49; subtle, 63. See also *Sapiṇḍa*
Bou-bhāt, 50
Brahma-cārī ("student"), 60
Brahmans, 5, 36, 54, 58, 59–61, 103
Brahmavaivarta Purāṇa, 94

Caste, xiv, 36, 40, 103
Clan. See *Kula*
Code and substance: nondualism of, xiv, 19–20, 86
Code for conduct (*dharma*), xiii; of *ātmīya-svajana*, 32–34; of *jñāti*, 14; of *jñāti-kuṭumba*, 21; of *kuṭumba*, 16–17, 19, 31–32; of *parivāra*, 17–19, 28–31
Cognates, xvi

Cognatic kindred, 8
Consanguines, xvi, 8, 14 68–69, 83–84, 89
Cūḍā-karaṇa. *See* Tonsure ceremony
Culā ("cooking hearth"), as symbol, 18
Cultural system, definition of, xii–xiii

Ḍāka-nāma, 57, 72
Dāmpatya-prema. *See* Love, conjugal
Dattaka-putra. *See* Adopted son
Dāyabhāga, 118
Death, 39, 62–66, 92, 99; and impurity, 102–6
Delivery ceremony, 54–55
Dharma, 42; definition of, 14
Dharma-bon, 80
Dharma-mā, 33
Dhṛti-homa, 49
Dīkṣā. *See* Initiation for release
Dumont, Louis, 68
Durgā-pūjā, 19, 23

Ear-piercing, ceremony of, 58–59
Eight beans (or cowries), ceremony of, 57
Eka-deha. See *Sapiṇḍa*
Eka-śarīra. See *Sapiṇḍa*
Ekoddiṣṭa. See *Śrāddha*s

Family: conjugal, 6; elementary, 6; extended, 6; joint, xvi, 6, 7, 64, 119–20; maximal, 6, 14–15, 74, 79, 84; minimal, 5–6; minimal, and kinship terms, 70, 73, 79, 84; nuclear, xvi, 6. See also *Parivāra*
Final rites, 39, 62–63. See also *Śrāddha*s
First feeding, ceremony of, 57–58
First outing, ceremony of, 56
Food, as symbol, 18, 33, 49, 50, 52, 63–64, 118
Fortes, Meyer, 35–36
Foster son, 32
Friends, 33, 117
Funeral. *See* Final rites

Gāe halud, 41
Garbhādhāna. *See* Impregnation, first, ceremony of
Gātra-haridra. See *Gāe halud*
Gāyatrī, 60
Generation: and kinship terms, 69, 71; and love, 25–26
Ghurye, G. S., 68
Gift-giving, 16–17, 19, 31, 44, 58, 81, 120
Goṣṭhī, 4, 8, 19, 119
Gotra, 4–5
Gotraja, 15
Gotra-parivartana, 48
Gṛha ("house"), 7
Gṛhastha ("householder"), 39, 45–46, 92
Gupta-nāma, 57
Guru, 61–62
Guru-bhāi, 33, 80
Guru-jana, 26
Guru-mā, 80

Hāte-khaḍī. *See* Beginning of study, rite of
Household, 7–8, 17–18, 29–30, 32–33
Householder. See *Gṛhastha*

Impregnation, first, ceremony of, 51–54
Impurity, birth, 106; death, 102–6
Inheritance. See *Parivāra*, division of
Initiation for release, rite of, 33, 61–62
Initiation into Vedic learning, rite of, 59–60

Jāmāi-ṣaṣṭhī, 19
James, E. O., 37–38
Jāta-karma. *See* Parturition ceremony
Jāti, xiv
Jimutavāhana, 118
Jñāti, 8–15, 74–80, 119; code for conduct of, 14, 17–19; defining features of, 13–15, 17, 19–21;

distant, terms for 79–80, 95; par excellence, 9, 14–15; residual, 9–12
Jñāti-bāndhava, 117
Jñāti-kuṭumba, 4, 8–9, 95; defining feature of, 21, 86–87
Jñāti-sambandhī, 117
Jñātitva. See *Jñāti*, code for conduct of
Joking, 31–32

Kāla-rātri, 50
Kanyā-dāna, 16, 43–44
Karṇa-vedha. *See* Ear-piercing, ceremony of
Kartā ("master"), 6–7, 18, 29–31; *baṛo*, 8; *mejo*, 8
Karve, Irawati, 68
Kāyasthas, 58
Kin, classes of: *ātmīya-svajana*, 3–4, 32–34, 96; *bāndhava*, 95–96, 117–18, 119; *jñāti*, 8–12, 95; *jñāti-kuṭumba*, 4, 8–9, 95; *kuṭumba*, 8–9, 15–17, 95–96; *sapiṇḍa*, 13–14, 104–7
Kinship: American, 8–9, 12, 17, 19, 86–87, 89, 91; Bengali, xii; Bengali conception of, 92–93; fictive, 32–33, 88–89; Muslim and Hindu, xi–xii, 99–100
Kinship terminology, patterns in, 68–69, 75, 77, 82–84, 89–91, 100–101
Kinship terms: basic, 70–74; definition of, 67–68; for abnormal relationships, 73–74; for *jñāti*, 74–80; for *kuṭumba*, 80–81; in Bengali and Sanskrit, 69–70; Muslim, 100–101
Kula ("clan"), 4–5, 8, 19; father's, 4, 9, 12, 13, 15, 118; husband's, 5, 9, 48–49; and kinship terms, 75–78; and marriage, 40, 45, 48, 49, 50; mother's father's, 4, 9–12, 13, 15, 118; Muslims, 99–100; priest of, 5, 36, 43, 45, 59, 102, 120–21
Kula-jāta, 95
Kula-purohita. See *Kula*, priest of
Kullūka Bhaṭṭa, 117, 119
Kuśaṇḍikā, 45–50
Kuṭumba, 8–9, 12, 80–81, 95–96, 119; code for conduct of, 16–17, 19, 31–32; defining features of, 15–17, 19–20; par excellence, 15–16; residual, 16
Kuṭumbitā. See *Kuṭumba*, code for conduct of

Lāja-homa, 46
Leaf, Murray J., 68
Life-stages, codes for conduct of, 39, 45–46, 60
Love: Bengali conception of, 21–22, 87–88; of brothers and sisters, 24–25; conjugal, 23–24, 72; egalitarian, 22–25, 87, filial, 26–29, 46, 71, 72; fraternal, 22–23; hierarchical, 25–29, 73, 87; parental, 26–29, 46, 72

Madan, T. N., 68
Madhuparka, 43
Manu, 117, 118, 119
Marriage: and love, 23–24; as defining feature, 15–16
Marriage ceremony: and caste, 40; anointment with turmeric, 41; changing of wife's *gotra*, 48; consummatory marriage, 51; gift of the bride, 43–44; leftover marriage, 44; six segments of, 40–41; structure of 42, 91–92; subsequent marriage, 44–50; touching wife's rice, 50; variations in, 39–40; walking of seven steps, 47–48
Mātṛ-bandhu, 118
Mātṛ-kula. See *Kula*, mother's father's
Medhājanana, 56
Medhātithi, 117, 118, 119
Menstruation, 51
Mitākṣarā, 13, 118
Monism, xiv, 32, 65–66, 86, 89

Mukhe-bhāt. See First feeding, ceremony of
Mukherjee, Bhabananda, 68
Mukhopādhyāya, Bhūdeva, 64–65
Mukti ("release"), 33, 61

Nāma-karaṇa. See Naming ceremony
Naming ceremony, 57
Nāndīmukha. See *Śrāddha*s
Neighborhood relations, 33
Niṣkramaṇa. See First outing, ceremony of
Nondualism. *See* Monism

Offspring, sex determination of, 54

Pādya, 43
Pāka-sparśa, 50
Pālita-chele. See Foster son
Pañcagavya, 52
Pañcāmṛta, 54
Parents, as gods, 26–28
Parivāra ("family"): code for conduct of, 17–18, 29–31, 87–88; definition of, 5–7, 8; division of, 64–65, 92, 118–19
Parivāra-varga ("bodily dependents"), 6–7
Parturition ceremony, 55–56
Pati-kula. See *Kula*, husband's
Patrilineage, See *Kula*
Piṇḍa. See Body; Food
Pitṛ-bandhu, 118
Pitṛ-kula. See *Kula*, father's
Prajāpati, 42
Preta-śarīra. See Body, departed
Prītija, 94–95, 96
Procreation, Hindu theory of, 52–54
Puberty: and initiation, 59; and marriage, 44, 51
Puṃ-savana. See Son, procreation ceremony for
Punar-vivāha, 51

Raghunandana Bhaṭṭācārya, 39, 102, 118–19
Rebirth, 62–66, 103
Relationship (*samparka*), 3, 17, 32–33, 92–93
Return home, rite of, 60

Sacraments. See *Saṃskāra*s
Sādh. See Delivery ceremony
Sagotra, 4
Śāktas, 36
Sakulya, 4, 15, 104–5
Samānodaka, 15, 104–5
Samāvartana. See Return home, rite of
Sambandha, 16, 94–95
Sambandha-nirṇaya, 96–98
Sambandhī, 16, 80, 119
Sampradāna, 42–44
Saṃsāra, 18
Saṃskāra, meaning of term, 37
Saṃskaras ("life cycle rites"): and Christian sacraments, 37–38; and impurity, 103–4; names and sequence of, 38–39, 58–59; preparatory acts for, 41–42; as symbolic acts, 35–36; variations in, 36–37
Sannyāsī ("ascetic"), 39
Sapiṇḍa, 3, 13–15, 20, 40, 104–7, 118–19. *See also* Body
Sapiṇḍīkaraṇa. See *Śrāddha*s
Sapta-padi gamana, 47–48
Sarma, Jyotirmoyee, 68
Ṣaṣṭhī, goddess of children, 51, 56–57
*Śastra*s, 36
Śavadāha. See Body, dead, cremation of
Schneider, David M., xii–xiii
Seed, 4, 37, 39, 64, 99
Seed and field, metaphor of, 52, 54
Semen, 22, 52–54, 104, 118
Servants, 32
Sex: and kinship terms, 69, 70–71; and love, 22–25, 26
Sharing, 17–19, 29–31, 80–81
Sīmantonnayana. See Delivery ceremony
Sindūra-dāna, 49–50

Snāna. See Return home, rite of
Snātaka, 61
Sneha. See Love, parental
Son, procreation ceremony for, 54
*Śrāddha*s, 39, 42, 63–64, 92
Strī-ācāra. See Women's rites
Śubha-dṛṣṭi, 43
Śubha-rātri, 51
Substance (*dhātu*), xiii
Śūdras, 39, 58, 59, 103, 106–7
Svajana, 3
Svāmī ("master"), 6–7, 67–68
Svāmī-kula. See *Kula*, husband's
Symbolic actions, xv–xvi, 17–18, 35–36, 91
Symbols, xiv–xv

Tadbhava, 69
Tatsama, 69
Tattva, 19
Tonsure ceremony, 58–59
Turner, Victor, 36

Upanayana. See Initiation into Vedic learning, rite of
Uttara-vivaha, 44–50

Vaiṣṇavas, 36
Vaṃśa, 4, 5, 49, 51
Vānaprastha ("hermit"), 39
van Gennep, Arnold, 35
Varṇa, 103
Vatuk, Sylvia, 68
Vidyāja, 94–95, 96
Vidyārambha. See Beginning of study, rite of
Vidyāratna, Kālīprasanna, 39
Vijayā-daśamī, 23
Vijñāneśvara, 13, 118
Village relations, 33
Vivāha. See Marriage; Marriage ceremony
Vṛddhi. See *Śrāddha*s

Widow, 64
Wife, as half-body of husband, xiv, 46, 48, 64, 78, 92, 99
Women's rites, 42, 44, 125

Yājñavalkya, 13, 118
Yonija, 94–95